ED ROSSBACH

Published in 1990 by Lark Books
50 College Street
Asheville, North Carolina, U.S.A. 28801

Copyright © 1990, Lark Books

Text copyright © 1990, The Textile Museum

Art Director: Rob Pulleyn
Production: Thom Boswell
Photography (unless otherwise noted): Jacques Gael Cressaty

ISBN 0-937274-52-6

Library of Congress Cataloging-in-Publication Data
Rossbach. Ed.
    Ed Rossbach: 40 years of exploration and innovation in fiber art/
    edited by Ann Pollard Rowe and Rebecca A.T. Stevens.
        p.   cm.
    Includes bibliographical references.
    ISBN 0-937274-52-6
    1. Rossbach, Ed—Themes, motives.   2. Fiberwork—United
States—History—20th century.   3. Textile fabrics—United States—
History—20th century.   I. Rowe, Ann P.   II. Stevens, Rebecca A.T.
III. Title.
NK8998.R68A4   1990
746'.092—dc20   89-83928
                                                            CIP

First Printing

1. **Double-Cloth Fabric,** 1949
   Cotton, rayon
   Double-cloth
   26" x 19"
   Collection of the Artist

ED ROSSBACH

40 YEARS OF EXPLORATION AND INNOVATION IN FIBER ART
Edited by Ann Pollard Rowe and Rebecca A.T. Stevens
1990 Washington, D.C. Exhibition Curated by Jane Fassett Brite

Lark Books
Asheville, North Carolina

The Textile Museum
Washington, D.C.

ACKNOWLEDGEMENTS

The Textile Museum is delighted to present in this volume the first overview of the life and work of Charles Edmund (Ed) Rossbach with discussions on his career as a teacher, writer, textile innovator, and most importantly, fiber art pioneer. Although we are able to illustrate only a fraction of the art works he has created over the last four and one-half decades, the photographs have been chosen to highlight Rossbach's use of innovative materials, his exploration of long-neglected historical textile structures, and his insightful, often humorous, commentary on our twentieth-century culture.

The Textile Museum has concurrently organized an exhibition of the works shown in this book which will circulate to museums across the country. When the exhibition closes and the objects have been returned to their owners, this book will remain as a permanent record of the expression and contribution of this extraordinary artist.

A project of this scope depends on the enthusiasm and vision of many. First, let me thank Ed Rossbach and his wife, Katherine Westphal, for their painstaking and thoughtful support, for hours spent fielding our questions, helping us locate art works and personal photographs, and for checking the accuracy of the information presented here. Second, I want to offer special thanks to Rebecca A. T. Stevens, coordinator of the Rossbach Retrospective exhibition and co-editor of this volume. Without her unfailing perceptiveness and persuasiveness this project would not have been realized. She has provided the structure which has enabled the many people involved to lend their talent and support.

The objects for the exhibition and illustrations in this book were selected by the exhibition curator, Jane F. Brite, who drew upon her long-standing friendship with Rossbach in preparing her essay on the artist's life. My thanks to Lia Cook for reflecting on Rossbach as a teacher, and to Nancy Corwin for sharing her studies in the field and helping define Rossbach's place in the world of fiber artists. Particular thanks are due Ann P. Rowe, Curator of Western Hemisphere Collections at The Textile Museum. Her analysis of Rossbach's use of textile structures and techniques calls upon us to recognize, understand and perceive his work within the panoply of historic textiles.

A volume of this nature needs the hand of someone with a sensitivity to the subject matter and the skill to craft a book in which image and word are balanced. We are fortunate to have had someone of this nature in Rebecca Caldwell, our copy editor. My thanks to the staff at Nine Press for attending to every detail of production and to Ann Rowe for her help at every step along the way.

The research was greatly assisted by the timely compilation of interviews with Ed Rossbach by the Oral History Project of the Bancroft Library of the University of California at Berkeley and by Peggy Whitney Hobbs, whose primary research was very helpful, Nancy Neumann Press for assistance in locating an important photograph, Barbara Okun for identifying Rossbach baskets in private collections, Bob and Charlotte Kornstein for first alerting the Museum to the superb Rossbach collection of Mr. and Mrs. Sanford Besser, and Michael Miller who assisted with locating works as well as the logistics of photographing, transporting, storing and shipping art works.

We are indebted to the public and private collectors who have generously lent their pieces to the exhibition and also given their permission to publish them.

The beautiful photography of the objects should be credited to Jacques Gael Cressaty, as well as Richard Eells, Mark Katzman, Franko Khoury, and Vince Foster.

Virtually everyone on The Textile Museum staff has played a part in ensuring the success of this enterprise. To each of you I extend my thanks for sharing the vision and being part of a ground-breaking enterprise both for The Textile Museum and the field of contemporary fiber art.

It is said that an object in motion tends to stay in motion, but in the case of a project such as this one it would not have been in motion long without the help of two Textile Museum trustees, Sheila Hicks and Jack Lenor Larsen, and the financial support of members of the Rossbach Retrospective Support Group whose names are listed in the Appendix. The National Endowment for the Arts, a Federal Agency, has generously supported the retrospective and publication, funding for which we are most grateful.

Finally, my most profound thanks to Samuel and Eleanor Rosenfeld, who founded the Rossbach Retrospective Support Group on behalf of The Textile Museum, and to Carl and Nancy Gewirz who expressed the first interest in this undertaking. We dedicate this book to these four far-sighted patrons.

Ursula Eland McCracken
Director
The Textile Museum
March 1990

2. **Clothing Fabric,** 1947
Wool
Plain weave
76 1/2" x 35 1/2"
Collection of the Artist

3. **Dark Indian,** 1987
   Mexican bark paper, palm leaves, commercial fabric
   Folded, stapled, heat transfer printed
   4 1/2″ x 9 1/2″ x 9 1/2″
   Collection of the Artist

TABLE OF CONTENTS

INTRODUCTION
Jack Lenor Larsen

Now, as an established fabric designer in New York City and a board member of The Textile Museum in Washington, D.C., it seems hard to believe that I was Ed Rossbach's graduate assistant in Seattle—forty short years ago. Even then, I admired his unique concern with broad ranges of fabric techniques. His was an artist's approach, drawn from his experiences as painter and potter. His work—then as now—was playfully experimental as it was scholarly. More than anything else it was his **own** poetic probing, of this time but quite outside the directions others were taking. (Most of us strove to be handmaidens to the new architecture, or to have some influence on fabric design.) With detachment, Rossbach listened to another drum. His own.

Although I was not his student (and he tended not to meddle with the career directions of those who were), he guided me well. First with encouragement, then with a recommendation to teach at the Seattle Art Museum, and later to apply for graduate study at Cranbrook Academy of Art. He was, then, the bow that sprung this arrow far and straight—towards a rewarding vocation.

As for Rossbach, the keen curiosity of this dean of American textiles led him to probe the fabric expressions from all of time. He looms as a giant straddling the present and those remote epochs when an emerging Mankind fashioned the first fiber elements into mats and baskets. He has at least considered most fabric structures from the eras in between—from primitive twining and braiding to complex bobbin laces, and the intricate decadence of paisley shawls. All materials, all cultures, all approaches to fabrics and the attitudes toward them fascinate him. He is not aloof from the images of Pop culture, nor from recycling such discarded materials as newspaper or mundane plastic sheeting. Most of his life he was also an educator, a great one, and the concerned dean of graduate studies in decorative art at Berkeley. We wonder how one man could have already achieved so much. To understand this we must comprehend what he did **not** do. He did not accept commissions (when many were available) or lectures, committee work or a bourgeois lifestyle, or in short, any activities that would have led to remuneration or success as it is commonly misunderstood. He is (repeatedly) ''the bear who went to the top of the mountain, to see what he could see.'' But having perceived what was on the other side, and what could be gained from exploiting it, he quickly descended . . . only to scale another height. In all this he is supported by the candid opinions and parallel energies of an even more freewheeling and irreverent artist: his wife, Katherine Westphal.

Because Ed Rossbach's teachings, writings, and prolific body of work have touched many and are so unspecific in time as to influence fabric attitudes in the next millennia, he is our colossus. He demonstrates the potential springboard of historical textiles to catapult us into a future still unknown. In the classic sense, his far reaching poetic vision is in the forefront of science, technology, and even to the reappraisal of textile history. He is awed by all those who have worked in these areas before—but not overly awed. Empathetic with their concerns and ambitions, he often as not attempts to meet their challenge, in his own terms. Let us follow this fellow who follows his dreams.

4. **African Congo Weaving I,** 1952
   Natural raffia
   Herringbone twill
   39″ x 35″
   Collection of the Artist

5. **African Congo Weaving II,** 1952
   Natural raffia, dyed shredded raffia, tules
   Herringbone twill
   37″ x 25 1/2″
   Collection of the Artist

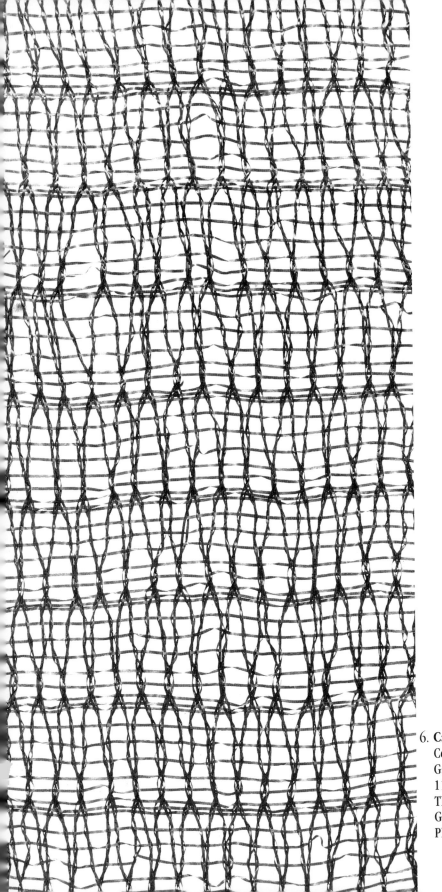

6. **Casement**, 1951 (detail)
Cellulose ribbon
Gauze weave
114″ x 37 1/2″
The Brooklyn Museum
Gift of Jack Lenor Larsen
Photo: William Lyall

ED ROSSBACH
Jane Fassett Brite with Rebecca Caldwell

In a career that has spanned more than four decades, Ed Rossbach has created consequential and influential work in every area of fiber art that he has explored, finding wonder in both the creation and study of the simplest and the most complex textile objects. Few materials or textile structures have escaped his notice. On the most pedestrian products of everyday life, such as newspaper, to the most elegant, Rossbach has practiced his powers to reinterpret and recreate, deftly employing the most elementary interlacing technique or the most complicated supplementary weft patterning, and often in the most unexpected manner. In fact, the ordinary transformed and made extraordinary is the essence of Rossbach—his life and his art.

THE EARLY YEARS

Charles Edmund Rossbach was born in 1914 and grew out of beginnings that were commonplace to many American families in the early years of this century. The grandchild of immigrants, Rossbach has a family history with chapters marked by movement and characterized by restlessness and change. His paternal grandparents immigrated from Germany, settling first in Chicago, where they had a small farm on the outskirts of the city alongside the Chicago River. Rossbach learned little of his father's family history except that after the legendary Chicago fire they went to South Dakota, where they hoped to succeed at farming. Rossbach's grandfather was a tinsmith by trade who was equipped with little else than the desire to farm land of his own. Lacking the background, his efforts at farming were thwarted. His resolve dampened by the harsh Dakota winters, his wife's by the relentless winds, he moved his family back to Chicago.[1] Rossbach's maternal grandparents, "sort of Scotch-Irish-English," according to Rossbach, had tried homesteading in upstate New York and Canada, where Rossbach's mother was born, before they, too, settled in Chicago. His parents met in Chicago and lived after their marriage at the very edge of the city in the suburb of Edison Park. The couple had four children: Doris, Ruth, Ed and Jane.

Being the only boy in what Rossbach describes as a supportive yet reserved family shaped early his sense of quiet self-sufficiency and self-containment, reinforced by the openness of the surrounding landscape: "[Ours was] the last house and we could look out the bedroom windows and there were just plains growing, just on the edge of things, and yet the whole thing was divided up in streets and sidewalks. It was a subdivision really, they called it, and yet there was nothing there. There was just the sensation of the plains"(OH, 5).

Rossbach remembers his father as not openly demonstrative nor communicative. At the same time, he maintains, his father was absolutely devoted to the family: "I remember he filled out a form once and he had to say what his hobbies were and he said his family. Well, this was true. This was his hobby and this was his life and at the same time I didn't know him at all"(OH, 1). Rossbach's mother was much more expressive, especially when she reminisced with her several sisters about the "old things," their childhood and their many colorful relatives. Recalling the hours spent listening to their lively talk, Rossbach said, "You got the whole structure of the family and I just *loved* that, just absolutely loved it"(OH, 2). The sense of family structure was reinforced by his grandmother's coming to live near them and by the frequent visits of his favorite aunt, Mary Jane, who worked at that time in a medical office in Michigan. The only one in her family to have travelled to Europe, she fascinated her young nephew with her involved stories about the people she worked with and about the time she spent in France as a Red Cross nurse during World War I.

Perhaps the earliest exposure to the first of the many textile techniques that would intrigue Rossbach came from his grandmother and her tatting. She tatted edging on handkerchiefs and then gave them as Christmas presents. The handkerchiefs served little usefulness except to convey to Rossbach a sense of their real value:

> I think maybe it was my first contact with textiles as being valuable beyond themselves. I think we knew at the time that these were old-fashioned and people didn't want little edgings on handkerchiefs any more . . . and yet you valued them because she had done them. I think that is still part of my feeling about textiles, that the work is very important to this thing and you are aware that somebody made this.(OH, 4)

The memory of his grandmother's delicate handwork remained with him, inspiring him in his later years to make his own 'amusing' attempts at tatting. 'I mean what an absurd thing,' he exclaimed during a recent interview. "I'm an old man sitting here learning how to tat from a book! It's the absurdity of it and that's the fun of it"(OH, 5). He laughed off his unsuccessful later attempts to teach the technique to students in a class of non-loom textiles. But the

7. **Tule Screen,** 1954 (detail)
   Tule, African reeds, viscose rayon, wool, cotton
   Plain weave, supplementary weft
   66 1/2″ x 37″
   Collection of the Artist

memory conveys a clear sense of those forces which characterize the artist's sensibility: the quiet and careful observation, the compelling curiosity to learn, and then the pure "joy of doing."

Among Rossbach's earliest recollections of something he crafted himself was a raffia teapot trivet. He remembers carefully weaving the raffia in and out of cardboard and presenting the finished trivet to his mother as a Christmas gift, which she treasured and used throughout her life.[2] He next recalls producing a card-table cloth with three designs blockprinted in each corner, which he also presented to his mother. The impetus for taking up this project was inspired by the sight of his sisters embroidering luncheon cloths which came with pre-stamped or iron-on patterns. The hard work intrigued him as did the idea of the heat-transferred designs, but these activities seemed somehow unacceptable play for a boy. As with his grandmother's tatting, however, the memory would become one day the inspiration to experiment, the constraints the invitation to rebel. Attributing his absorption with heat transfers to this early introduction, Rossbach states, "It's as though I have picked up on all of this stuff that was going on that was forbidden to me"(OH, 7).

Erector Sets, Tinker Toys, and Lincoln Logs were instead the toys of his boyhood, and with them he built "not wildly elaborate structures like those in the catalogs, but simple constructions, over and over." He says, "I feel that this interest is incorporated in my textiles"(OH, 7). The textile techniques that were sanctioned for his sisters in their youth have never really found a place in Rossbach's later work: "Ever since that early time," he recalls, "I have felt uncomfortable doing anything like sewing, darning, appliqueing, embroidering. I avoid them in my own work as somehow not appropriate activity for a man. Knitting also. Any of the textile techniques that my sisters did"(OH, 7).

EARLY ARTISTIC INFLUENCES

The Rossbach family moved several times throughout these early years. In 1922, when Rossbach was eight years old, his family moved from Chicago and settled first in Seattle until 1924 and then in Tacoma, Washington, from 1924 until 1928. In 1928 they moved back to Illinois. The fourteen-year-old Rossbach entered Lyons Township High School in LaGrange, where he soon met two of the most influential teachers in the development of his career as an artist. These two teachers recognized and encouraged his talents in art and writing.

The more flamboyant of the two was Edith Blaisdell Murphy, an art teacher who fostered his creativity all through high school. She was a maverick and wonderful eccentric. She organized the *All Arts Klub,* a club through which she encouraged the members to raise money selling hot dogs at the high school games in order to take trips to the Art Institute of Chicago. The outings were all engineered to have the children experience the city and introduce them to the fine arts. They viewed exhibitions, attended lectures, and went to plays and musicals.

At LaGrange, Murphy produced the annual club performances which she adapted from the most unlikely sources, chosen primarily because of their interesting and elaborate demands for costumes and settings. Rossbach recalls the productions as "just awful things for your family to have to sit through. . . . We were so bad!" he laughs, "I mean everybody knew they were just terrible, but there we were"(OH, 11). However ostentatious and amateur the productions were, they fostered a budding interest in costume design and fabrics for the young student and an abiding love of the theatre.

The irrepressible Mrs. Murphy rewarded her students by allowing them to spend their study hall time in the art room, an opportunity that Rossbach and his fellow art students made ample use of. Murphy's influence also motivated Rossbach to take a Saturday class in drawing at an art school in Chicago.

Kate Smith was the other important teacher during Rossbach's years in LaGrange. She was very supportive of his other outstanding talent, writing, encouraging him to write for the high school newspaper, which he happily did. No other teacher prior to Smith, he recalls, had ever expressed any interest in his writing nor encouraged him to develop his abilities. Her English class was a ''wonder,'' requiring the not-so reluctant Rossbach to read Shakespeare and ''the best that had been written.'' From that point on, teachers singled out his abilities, and he began to write seriously, mindful of how difficult and labored a process it is, yet one that is so full of ''possibilities.''(OH, 11-13)

A good deal of his remaining free time in his high school years was spent in the school library, where Rossbach assisted the librarian with shelving and cataloging books. The unlimited access to books and

8. Ed with his sisters Ruth (left) and Doris (right), ready for the Fourth of July parade in Edison Park, Illinois, about 1919.

the librarian who guided his reading to a certain extent directed Rossbach to delve early into ambitious subjects. Most of his reading from that time, he realizes, was socially oriented, steering him toward books on the Russian Revolution and the five-year plans as well as on the predicament of blacks in the United States.[3]

The Depression took its toll on the Rossbach family as it did on so many others of the time. When Rossbach's father lost his job, the family did what so many other families did; they piled all their belongings into the car and moved to what they hoped would be a better place where more jobs were available. Their destination was Seattle, Washington, where they returned in 1931 to live with his mother's sister, Lou, and her husband. This uncle was a postal worker and the only family member at the time holding a job. The close-knit, supportive family helped each other during these difficult years, and they lived with Aunt Lou for what seemed to Rossbach a very long time. Eventually his sister Doris, a trained librarian, found employment as did his sister Ruth, who was an office worker.

During the years his family lived with his aunt and uncle, Rossbach developed his first interest in quilting. His sisters and mother set up quilting frames in the basement and quilted in the evening. Rossbach would often sit with them while they quilted and sometimes read aloud to them. Although he himself never practiced the technique, Rossbach always admired it, and perhaps from his admiration and his nostalgia, he conceived of the idea for **Vinyl Log Cabin** in 1970 (Fig. 45). He used the court house steps pattern, and, with vinyl heat-sealed flagging tape, he created an unusual and typically Rossbach adaptation of the technique.

When they were young adults finding their way in Seattle, Rossbach's sister Ruth bought a second-hand loom. Describing it as a very bad one, Rossbach nevertheless was interested in how the loom worked and wove a little on it. The experience piqued his curiosity enough to sign up for a class in weaving at Broadway Night School.

Another experience around that time kindled his curiosity in weaving as well. In 1940 Rossbach went on an outing with his sisters to the International Exposition near San Francisco, California, and saw a decorative arts exhibit that Dorothy Liebes had there. He did not know anything about Dorothy Liebes prior to the trip, nor about how she was revolutionizing not only the idea of contemporary handweaving but the concept of "decorative arts."[4] He just knew that what he saw captured his interest and his curiosity. After seeing the exhibit, Rossbach wrote in his diary that he would like to learn how to weave so that he could produce upholstery material. He recalls now that he never did weave much upholstery and that which he did he never used, but the introduction to her work and to the contemporary textiles and weavings that she had collected for the installation was a significant one.

EDUCATION

The young artist who had made that declaration in his diary had just completed the Bachelor of Arts Degree in Painting and Design at the University of Washington in Seattle in 1940, the first of the three degrees he earned in his career. College had never been pushed in Rossbach's family, but there was always the assumption that he and his sisters would attend.[5] The concern for financial security after living through the Depression shaped Rossbach's early university years, however, and he interrupted his studies after his first two semesters to work at a Civil Service job in Spokane. The six months spent with that job would assure him of remaining on an active list of Civil Service candidates should he ever need a job for "security's" sake. He returned to the university on a Phi Beta Kappa Scholarship and was graduated in 1940 with Phi Beta Kappa and Magna Cum Laude honors.

Because of his high school art interests, Rossbach declared his major at the university in painting and design with the intention of becoming an art teacher. He studied painting there under Johannes Molzahn and Amedée Ozenfant, aware even then of his efforts to adapt to their approaches and to "please" them. (See Corwin/Stevens essay.) He was a diligent student in all respects, doing his work as assigned. So diligent, in fact, that he recalls, "I did what the teachers seemed to want me to be doing, and for the time being accepted their standards."[6] Of his early art training, he contends:

> I was never, in school or any where else, encouraged to work expressively. I felt that I was always doing assignments—they interested me, and I devoted my energies to them, but I seldom did 'art' apart from that, and what I did was most clearly related to what I had been taught: I never felt that the field was wide open, and that I could go in any direction I wanted to.[7]

The requisite courses of his English composition minor also frustrated him because of the lack of creative writing classes offered, but the few education courses he took proved unbearable. Refusing to take any further ones in that curriculum, he concluded that he wasn't "qualified" then to be a teacher.

Though studying at the university, he lived at home and continued to cultivate his interests in dance and the theatre that his high school teacher had awakened. The stacks of books arranged in sculptural columns around his bed attested to his avid interests.[8] And, while looking through one of his favorite volumes, which contained costume drawings for the ballet by Bakst, he followed the career of a local Seattle dancer, Marc Platoff, who was invited to join the Ballet Russe de Monte Carlo. Rossbach attended many ballets, particularly Russian ballets of the 1930s, and

was taken with their drama and exquisite costumes. More than anything, though, his avid interest and Platoff's career made him long to run away with the ballet, to do anything, "just to be involved."[9]

His fondness for the ballet and the theatre had earlier found another outlet of expression in a slightly different medium of performance. Rossbach had become intrigued with the art of puppetry after he and his sisters has seen a puppet show together in Seattle while still in high school. He began making his own marionettes and soon enlisted his whole family's participation in his project. Together they performed original puppet shows at churches and schools, driven from one performance to another by their father. His family still struggling to cope in the grips of the Depression's hardships, Rossbach fantasized about finding a means to save them, to provide a job for his father and for them all. The marionette show was his hoped-for solution to their hardships, and he began writing a book on how to make marionettes, illustrating it himself. Before entering college, he had sent the manuscript to the Harcourt Brace Publishing house, and, to his surprise and somewhat to his dismay, the book was accepted. His first book, *Making Marionettes,* was published in 1938, Rossbach's freshman year at the University of Washington. Because of his shyness, Rossbach was unable to acknowledge publicly that he was the author. In fact, he once told a fellow student that his uncle had written the book when she noted the author's same last name on the book jacket. During the war, he was asked to allow the copper printing plates to be melted down for the war effort, and he agreed.(OH, 17-18)

Continuing with his plans to teach eventually, Rossbach accepted a Romiette Stevens Scholarship in 1940 to Columbia University in New York, where a year later he would earn the Master of Arts degree in art education. "The idea of launching off to go to New York seemed very daring and it was just wonderful,"

Rossbach recalled(OH, 15). The program at Columbia was a progressive one for the times, which required course work combined with a year of practice teaching in all levels at the experimental school, Horace Mann. Once again, Rossbach found another very supportive teacher there who took him under her wing; the teacher, Belle Boas, is remembered by Rossbach as being "very urbane, kind of aloof and grand." Boas supervised the student teachers in art education at Columbia University; she arranged for her charges to meet working artists in their studios, and urged them to take full advantage of the city's rich cultural life. Her eager pupil visited museums and galleries, attended lectures and concerts, sat in on rehearsals of Martha Graham's company, went to the theatre and the opera, and would recall the year as "marvelous, really eye opening"(OH, 15).

Equipped with his new degree and his progressive pedagogy, Rossbach set out again for the West Coast and took on his first position, teaching seventh graders at a school in the small farm community of Puyallup located outside of Seattle. He recalled, "From the time I was teaching seventh grade, I felt the children were more knowledgeable than I was, and they *were*. I was teaching in a farm community and these kids were knowledgeable about a whole range of important things that I had absolutely no knowledge of whatsoever and it was always slightly uncomfortable"(OH, 19). His inability to stem the unruly behavior of a few disruptive students made the new teacher, never a firm disciplinarian, even more uncomfortable. His control of the classroom and his outlook improved with the second semester, but Rossbach still found it difficult to heed the advice given in the Columbia program to remain on the first job for two years.

THE ARMY AND THE ALEUTIAN ISLANDS

When the attack on Pearl Harbor occurred, he resigned his teaching post and went into the Army. He enlisted in order to be accepted into the Alaska Communications System, Signal Corps, where he learned Morse Code and how to take messages that were jumbled to confuse the Japanese. His typing skills got him reassigned to the personnel office for the next three years until he was sent to Adak in the Aleutian Islands for what turned out to be the last year of the war.

On Adak he became inspired by the island's grasses and tried to fashion them into baskets. Lacking the know-how to complete his forms, Rossbach asked his sister to send a Boy Scout manual on basketry in hopes of learning more about the process(OH, 22). Unfortunately, the manual could no longer be found, but the interest became a seed for future exploration which germinated and grew. He wrote later, describing the landscape and his first attempts:

> I set about gathering individual grasses and stalks which seemed promising although I had little idea what constituted quality in basketry materials. No information was available, for the Aleuts had been removed from their islands and, strangely, nothing of their culture was to be seen anywhere. It was as though hostile elements had furiously erased every mark of human existence and returned the land to something primeval, alien, and—despite the army which had alighted—uninhabited. . . . I found myself indulging in a solitary ritual of observation. The islands became for me, at least in retrospect, a land of dreams—various, beautiful, and new. I achieved no baskets, only a box of selected grasses and a brittle start of interweaving.[10]

The time in the Aleutian Islands was a stimulating and satisfying period for Rossbach. Stationed with an intelligent group of people who provided good company and conversation, he spent many enjoyable hours with them and on his own listening to classical music recordings and hiking along the beaches. He chronicled his impressions of the landscape in a series of drawings that he would complete inside his hut after retreating from the cold. A portfolio of these drawings won the corpsman acceptance to graduate school at Cranbrook Academy of Art in Bloomfield Hills, Michigan, at the war's end.[11]

CRANBROOK ACADEMY

Rossbach entered Cranbrook at mid-term in 1946 on the GI Bill. He chose the school because he was interested in crafts, and it was the premier program in craft studies at that time. Cranbrook officials thought he would be entering their painting program, based upon the strength of his portfolio. Instead, ceramics

9. Winter in Adak, Alaska, 1945. The quonset hut "Hotel Olympic", where Rossbach spent a year. Mt. Moffett in the background.

became his primary area of concentration and weaving the secondary. Weaving was rather rigidly structured at Cranbrook during Rossbach's student days. Teachers taught in the Scandinavian Modern traditions, and students were required to weave three-yard lengths of fabric which were considered prototypes for the textile industry. These assignments again seemed restrictive to Rossbach as he began his studies under Marianne Strengell.[12] Though he later paid tribute to the sensitivity of her weaving, saying she allowed the warp and weft to function almost "ideally," Rossbach was not to find her the most attentive of teachers. Her commitment at the time lay with her own work, Rossbach recalled, and she did not allow her students to visit her own studio at the rear of the teaching studio or to see her work. Although she referred to her approach to handweaving as being purely collaborative, the collaboration hinged on the relationship between the handweaver, the architect and industry. The students' role was almost incidental:

> The weaving taught at Cranbrook during the 40's was exclusively 'contemporary weaving.' Nothing else was permitted. A sort of formula for teaching evolved. . . . Looking back now, it appears that during the period when architects and handweavers collaborated, many of us who were not in any position to collaborate were playing at it, content to work within a remarkably narrow range of weaving possibilities, untroubled by any awareness of what was possible and wonderful in weaving, and untroubled too by the solemn restraints that somehow had been imposed upon us. Small wonder that in a few years a vigorous reaction occurred.[13]

Rossbach anticipated the 'vigorous reaction' to contemporary handweaving during his student days in Strengell's class at Cranbrook. At first he met the requirements to the letter, turning out his subtly-hued three-yard lengths, but his creative mind was wandering in experimental directions. He began to paint the warp, much to the consternation of Strengell, and the casement fabrics he wove using plastic are a first glimmer of his innovative use of materials to come.

Though fiber soon became the medium of choice for self-expression by Rossbach, he claims, "It was just an historical accident"(OH, 26). Most of his student energy and time at Cranbrook was spent in the ceramics department under the guidance of Maija Grotell. The fiber department was solely concerned with designing for industry, but the ceramics department under Grotell was dramatically different. She was much more personally involved with her students and sensitive to their needs. Crediting Cranbrook with establishing a foundation from which he could take off, Rossbach remembers Grotell as introducing him to the "wonder" of textiles: "Her response to textiles was so emotional, and so sensitive—it put textiles into another realm of meaning and expression"[14] (See Corwin/Stevens discussion.)

THE UNIVERSITY OF WASHINGTON AT SEATTLE

Rossbach was graduated from Cranbrook Academy of Art in 1947 with a Master of Fine Arts in Ceramics and Weaving. He returned that same year to teach at his undergraduate alma mater, the University of Washington at Seattle, where his appointment was split between two departments: the Art Department in which he taught painting and the Home Economics Department in which he taught weaving.

The Home Economics Department assigned a bright young student, Jack Lenor Larsen, who had been taking classes in interior decoration to be Rossbach's teaching assistant. Having Larsen as a teaching assistant was extremely helpful but a little nonplusing, according to Rossbach, because Larsen was so knowledgeable and so competent. Rossbach recalls that his ambitious assistant had enormous drive. Larsen, he says, "had fifty thousand things and interests going simultaneously. At the same time he was producing, and had private students, and you don't know how anybody would have that much energy"(OH, 33). This was the beginning of an important professional relationship that has lasted throughout the long and productive careers of both men.[15]

Certainly the most important and enduring relationship of Rossbach's life, both personal and professional, began while at the University of Washington in Seattle. Rossbach met his wife, Katherine Westphal, who at the time was also teaching in the painting department, and they were married in 1950. She had received her Bachelor of Arts and Master of Arts degrees in painting at the University of California, Berkeley, during the war years.[16]

A chance meeting in Seattle with Lea Miller, then head of the weaving program at Berkeley and a former teacher of Rossbach's at Seattle, resulted in the opportunity for Rossbach himself to make his way to Berkeley. Miller extended an invitation for Rossbach to teach a summer course on the California campus, an "audition" of sorts for the full-time position that was to be extended the following school year.[17] The invitation was a propitious one, and the summer was spent teaching weaving, renewing old acquaintances and cementing new alliances.

One acquaintance he renewed that summer was with Dorothy Liebes, whose pioneering work had enthralled him a decade earlier. This time Rossbach was to meet the artist herself when the Chairman of the Decorative Art Department at Berkeley, Winfield Scott Wellington, took Rossbach to visit Liebes' flourishing production studio in San Francisco. At the time, Rossbach did not know he was meeting the person who was responsible for the exhibition which had given him the desire to learn to weave. "Liebes created the studio as a setting for herself—she was the star. She always had style and flair in her own appearance and in her surroundings. Everyone who recalls the Liebes days mentions what a striking, stylish, tall blond woman she was. Those who knew her remember her as a lively personality with a talent for promotion."[18]

A ritual mid-morning coffee hour capped off the studio visit, wherein Liebes gathered all of her weavers and her guests in a large circle on the patio outside to talk about weaving. "It wasn't as though Dorothy Liebes was holding court," according to Rossbach. On the contrary, he thought her gathering more like a small seminar and its leader extremely sophisticated. He would note the irony of his eventually writing articles publicizing her achievements when, at the time of their meeting, she didn't show the slightest bit of interest in him(OH, 53).

THE UNIVERSITY OF CALIFORNIA AT BERKELEY

Rossbach joined the Decorative Art Department at Berkeley as Assistant Professor of Design in 1950. Six years later he became an Associate Professor, and six years after that he was promoted to full Professor. He retired from the university in 1979 with the distinguished rank of Professor Emeritus.

The three decades at Berkeley were extraordinarily productive for Rossbach, despite the distractions and the frustrations presented by political turmoil within and outside of the university. Some of Rossbach's most vivid recollections of his tenure there revolve around his department's ongoing struggle to establish

10. **Casement Cloth,** 1952 (detail)
Linen, mohair, viscose rayon
Gauze weave
107" x 31 1/2"
The Metropolitan Museum of Art,
Gift of the Artist, 1985
Photo: The Metropolitan Museum of Art

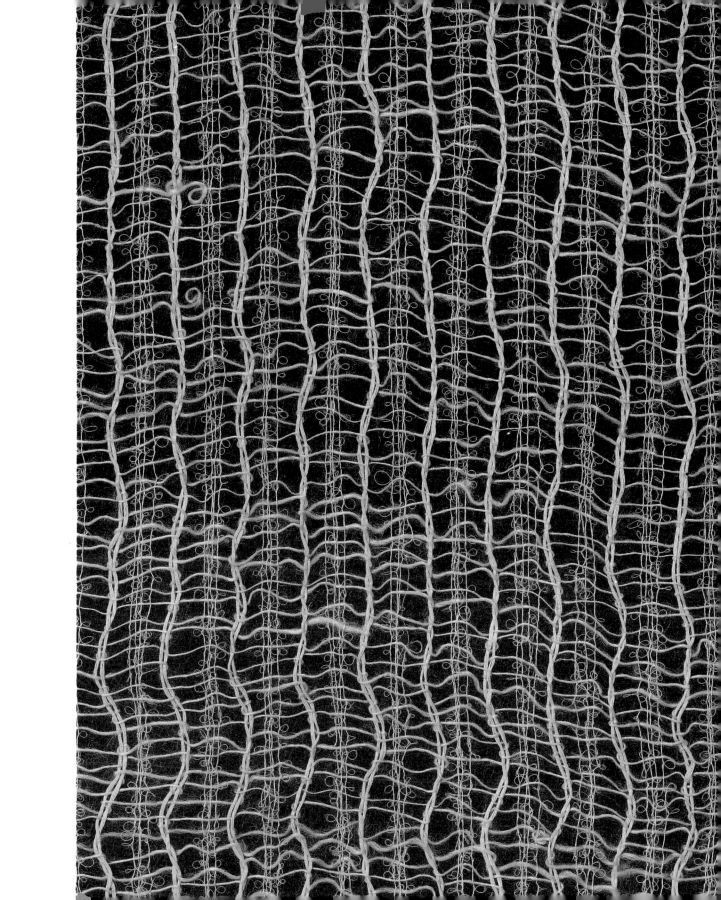

11. **Rug,** 1952
    Cotton, hemp
    Summer and Winter Weave
    (plain weave with supplementary weft)
    65″ x 38 1/2″
    Collection of the Artist

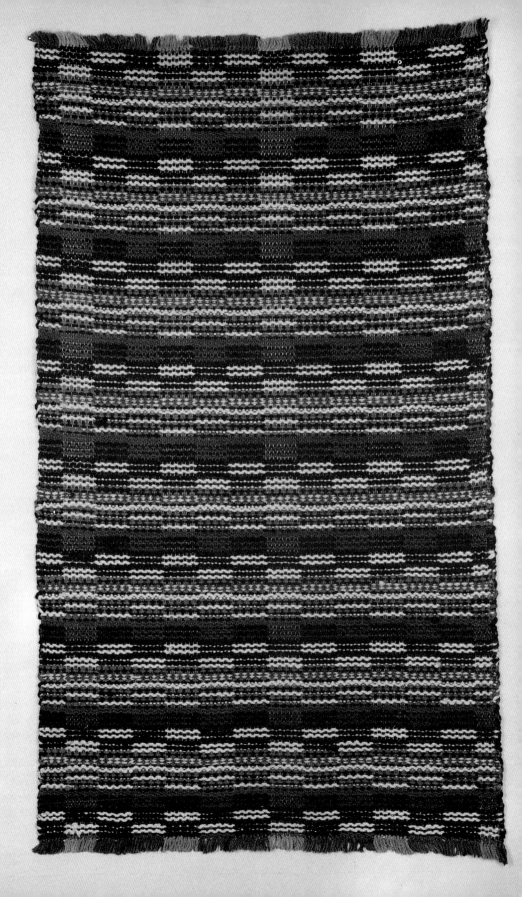

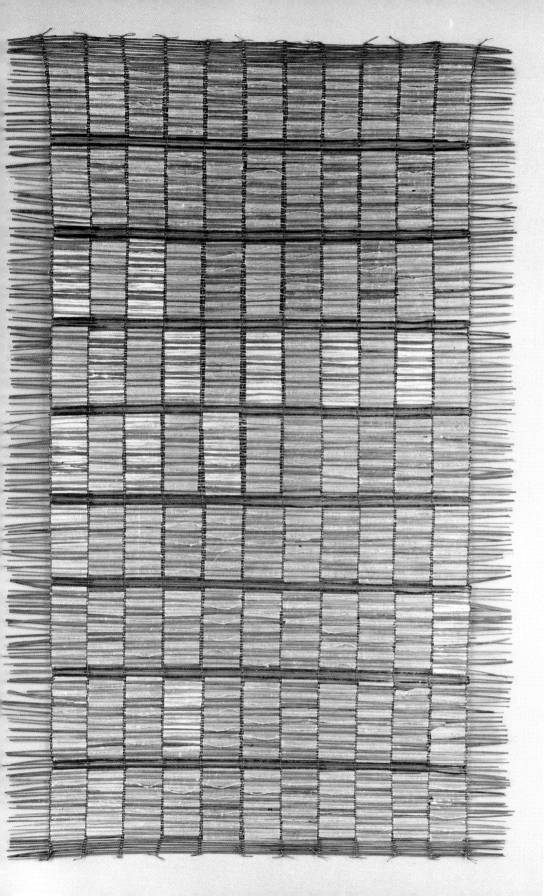

12. **African Reeds,** 1952
   Metallic paper, reeds, rayon, linen
   Warp twining
   34 1/2″ x 23″
   Collection of the Artist

23

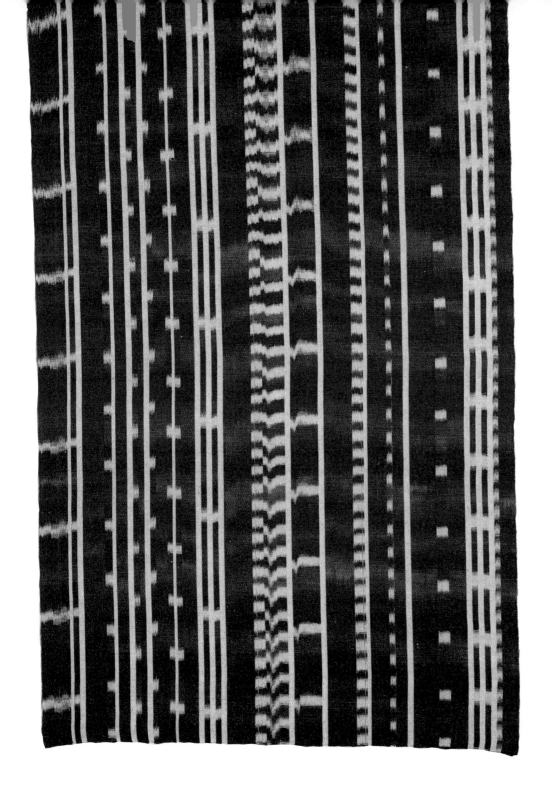

13. **Ikat,** 1956 (detail)
    Silk
    Plain weave, warp ikat
    99 1/2″ x 43″
    Collection of the Artist

14. **Double Ikat,** 1956 (detail)
    Silk
    Twill weave, warp and weft ika
    102″ x 38 1/2″
    Collection of the Artist

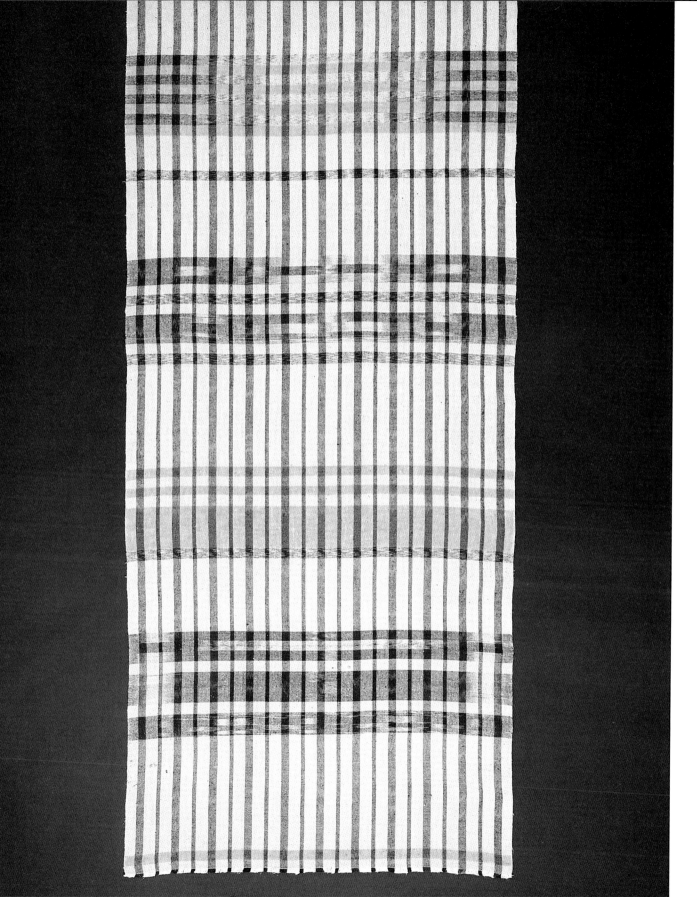

its own identity within the university. Turned out like a poor and somewhat disreputable relation from the College of Letters and Science, the Design Department (earlier known as the Decorative Art Department) was forced to form an uneasy alliance with the College of Environmental Design, becoming known in 1975 as the Program in Visual Design, and then was phased out entirely during the late 1970's.

Its faculty was made up of such luminaries in diverse disciplines over the years as Winfield Scott Wellington, Lila M. O'Neale, Anna H. Gayton, Mary Dumas, Lea van P. Miller, Rossbach, and, in the sixties, Peter Voulkos, Marvin Lipofsky, Imogene Gieling, Lillian Elliott, and Ranghild Langlet. Unfortunately the department's energies were focused, for the most part, on maintaining the inflexible academic standards set by the university often at the expense of artistic productivity. Rossbach characterizes the department as divided according to attitude, age and artistic output: "At the beginning when I came, there was just the old guard and the people willing to go along with the old guard . . . I respected what they were doing and it seemed the way things should be"(OH, 33). Yet Rossbach also realized the inherent obstacles posed by the 'old guard's' rigidity and proclivity to avoid risks. He found the atmosphere decidedly different from the openness nurtured by the faculty at Washington when he was there:

> I would be less than honest if I said that the adjustment from the University of Washington to UC Berkeley was not difficult. At Washington a group of young people, largely veterans, had been hired because of the unbelievable influx of students following the war. These new teachers were extremely dedicated and involved in art. We were painting, sometimes hiring a model and meeting as a group in the evening. It was a most stimulating milieu even though, at the university, we were required to teach unusually long hours, often on Saturday . . . In Berkeley, by contrast, there was an isolation which was very difficult to break through.[19]

The more familiar he became with the department's entrenched and ultimately unproductive administration, the more determined he was to cultivate the subjects of his own curiosity and to draw on and depart from traditional techniques in both his teaching and his artwork.

Rossbach's academic career progressed along an ideally prescribed path: he was promoted at the regular intervals, accorded sabbaticals and even awarded the department's Creative Arts Grant, which allowed him a year's respite from his teaching responsibilities to facilitate his artwork. "But at the same time," he said, "fundamentally there was no belief in what I was doing or what any of us were doing, and Katherine and I used to talk about this. We would just fantasize what a person could do that the administration of the University would value"(OH, 33).

Application forms for sabbaticals and other academic awards, designed as they were for the research efforts of the more conventional disciplines, reflected the university's inability to acknowledge creative work. Rossbach recalled the relief of his colleagues and himself upon learning that an application had been approved and funds awarded or a request for a sabbatical leave had been granted: "I always had the vague feeling that I was getting away with something, and that my contribution to the university was not

15. **Upholstery Fabric,** 1959 (detail)
Silk, rayon
Twill weave
96 1/2″ x 42 3/4″
The Metropolitan Museum of Art,
Gift of the Artist, 1985
Photo: The Metropolitan Museum of Art

16. **Stencilled Textile**, 1952-3
   Mexican handwoven cotton, dye
   Plain weave, stencilled
   123″ x 34 3/4″
   The Metropolitan Museum of Art,
   Gift of the Artist, 1985
   Photo: The Metropolitan Museum of Art

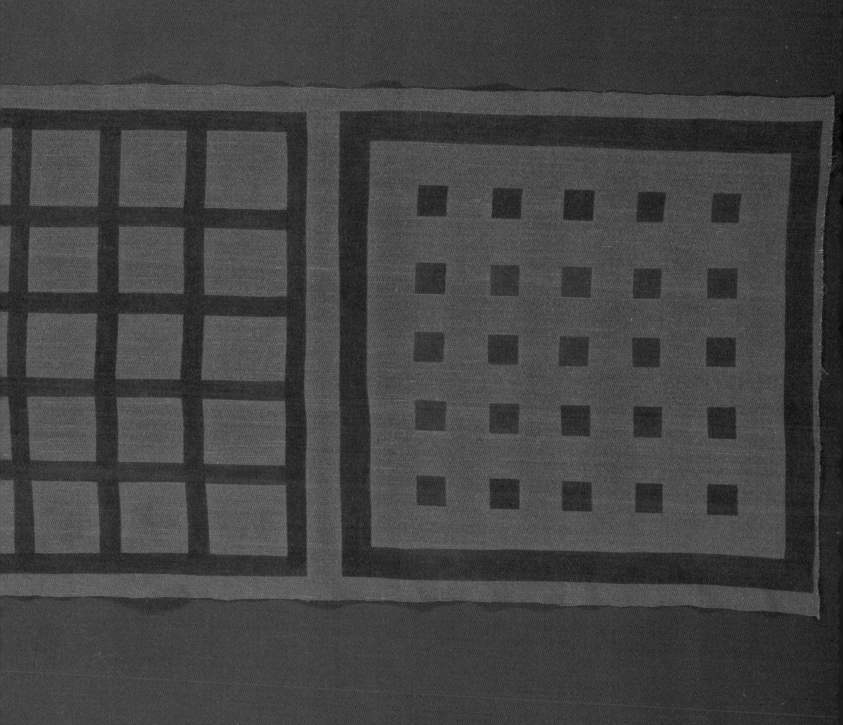

quite in the same league as that of faculty in Classics, English, or most especially, Science. But my leaves and grants always came through, and I felt most appreciative."[20]

Rossbach's prominent place on the department's faculty was never in dispute. Even in the early years after his arrival in Berkeley he was already bringing acclaim to the university through the publication of a number of articles on a range of textile techniques, through the many awards he began collecting beginning in the mid 40s, and through the variety of important group exhibitions for which his work was selected. Despite his academic accomplishments, and even after a stint as an administrator in the department, Rossbach kept himself removed from departmental politics. His considerable energies were instead channeled into the experimentation and observation, both in and out of the classroom, that the subjects of his own studies and those of his students were sparking.

The creative and political climate of Berkeley was then and has continued to be variably cloudy, sometimes stormy, and indeed never mild. While the name even today still conjurs up evening-news images of campus unrest, the area in and surrounding the university has always been home to a variety of tirelessly productive artists whose works can be counted upon to be intellectually and emotionally challenging. The Rossbachs were very much a part of this community, taking advantage of the area's many cultural opportunities. One program that attracted their interest was at Mills College in Oakland. Mills' thriving arts program attracted prominent painters, sculptors, musicians and other well-known guest artists each summer. The couple frequented musical events and shows

17. Katherine and Ed, Venice, Italy, 1960.

there, and regularly attended exhibitions of works from the graduate ceramics program there(OH, 49). Both Rossbach and Westphal remained heavily involved in ceramics, though not then taught at Berkeley, by taking night classes at the California College of Arts and Crafts. Rossbach remembers their being much more involved in the ceramics that was going on in the area than with any of the weaving.

The Rossbachs also spent an enjoyable part of their early years in Berkeley developing ideas and avenues for working on projects together. Some evenings during this time might have found them working, designing printed fabric for industry. Sitting down after dinner, they could produce often several designs in an evening, send the designs painted or batiked on cloth with measurements of their repeats off to their New York Agent, Frederick Karoly, and then await news via special delivery letter of their sale. The special delivery letters added excitement to the projects, but even more fun to the couple was keeping watch over fabric counters, seeing their designs appearing and people wearing them.[21] The Rossbachs wouldn't know necessarily to whom their designs had been sold, nor would they remember at times which of the two of them had actually produced which design(OH, 69-71).

KATHERINE WESTPHAL

The relationship of Rossbach and Westphal is indeed a marriage of the most vital and gracious kind, sustained at least in part over four decades together through the abiding respect that each fosters for the other's humanity and creativity. Rossbach credits Westphal with having much more confidence in his work than he allows himself. "It is a comfortable feeling," he describes, "that at least one person whose opinion I value, goes along with what I am doing."[22] While their creative outputs have become more and more dissimilar since the textile designs of their first

years together, the two share a dedication to each other and to craft that has kept them in constant motion and consistently creating. They faced early on the problems posed by dual careers and busy schedules, complicated even further for a period by long commutes when Rossbach taught at Berkeley and Westphal at the University of California at Davis, 60 miles apart.

They have coexisted productively and happily since before their retirement in a larger old home in Berkeley, complaining of a constant lack of adequate studio and storage space, yet always finding room for another toy collected on their travels or for the succession of dogs which they came to value far more than any of the possessions the dogs were acquired to guard. Very much a part of the household, the dogs hold a prominent place in the couple's shared symbolic vocabulary as well. Images of the dogs have appeared often in both their works, in Rossbach's brocaded silks, in Westphal's quilts, and in manipulated photographs.

The couple's fondness for remaining home with their mixed brood has come increasingly in conflict in recent years with their shared wanderlust, which has compelled them to travel extensively during sabbaticals and since their retirement. Their travels together have taken them through Europe, Asia and Africa as well as through parts of North and South America. Predictably, their attitudes toward travel and their manner of preparing for each trip are distinctly different. Not himself inclined to study in advance, Rossbach characterizes Westphal as the trip planner, checking out books from the library in preparation, and the trip archivist, documenting their journeys with her many photographs.[23] However reluctant he might be to carry a camera on recent travels, Rossbach credits the photographs with providing enjoyment "beyond belief" on their return home: "We spend much time looking at our prints, observing a multitude of details that we were unaware of when we were traveling . . . We dis-

18. **Bamako,** 1962 - 1963 (detail)
    Cotton
    2/1 Twill, silk screened warp
    80″ x 34 1/2″
    Ed Rossbach, designer
    Jack Lenor Larsen, Inc.,
        Manufacturer
    Jack Lenor Larsen, Inc.
    Photo: Franko Khoury

19. **Bamako,** 1960 (detail)
    Linen, silk
    Plain weave, painted warp
    80 1/2″ x 34 1/2″
    Courtesy of The Art Institute of
        Chicago
    Photo: The Art Institute of
        Chicago

cuss our prints and compare our observations, which are surprisingly different.'[24] Each does his or her own form of ''follow-up'' on their travels, with Westphal translating her experience into her artwork in perhaps a much more immediate manner. Rossbach's brand of follow-up differs in that questions and observations that arise while travelling are researched upon his return and are eventually reflected in his work. For instance, the ceramic vessels which were particularly intriguing to Rossbach on a journey to Banpo, a Neolithic site in China, are the subjects of his recent inquiries. When he is successful at locating information on the site, he is sure his baskets will ''reflect the shapes of these most ancient pots.''[25]

TRAVEL

The experience of travel has become for Rossbach a ''private and personal'' one, which does not much involve anyone other than himself and Westphal in the immediate experience of a destination. Unable to travel independent of a group in recent years, he expresses bewilderment of the people on organized tours: ''They never seem to express any excitement or curiosity about what they are seeing, while to me it is mindblowingly exciting. . . .''[26] However personal an ex-

20. **Wood Block and Resist,** 1960 (detail)
   Batiste cotton
   Wood block printed, batik
   124" x 36 1/2"
   Collection of the Artist

21. **Kasuri Heads III,** 1966
   Cotton
   Plain weave, weft ikat
   11" x 7 1/2"
   Collection of the Artist

perience travel has become, Rossbach does admit to missing the opportunity to share his observations with his students:

> In a very strange way, I always felt that I was sharing my sabbaticals, no matter what I was doing, with my students. What I experienced on these leaves had a profound, and often unpredictable, effect on my teaching. . . . I miss the opportunity to talk about the excitement of it all. I miss being able to show my slides, which I find I was really taking to show my students.[27]

His early sabbatical leaves were designed to have a direct connection to his classroom teaching. The young teacher determined, insofar as he was able, "not to be a teacher who had not experienced what he was talking about." Hence Rossbach dedicated his first sabbatical to experiencing directly the great art works of Europe which he had previously seen only in slides. And thereafter he was better able to lend validity to his exhortations for his students to experience art directly. He recalls, "When I found myself teaching with a faculty that was matter-of-fact about their travels, and who spoke familiarly about the great European museums, I was determined to travel, to catch up."[28]

Perhaps the least difficult part of the rigorous application process for sabbatical leave to Rossbach was the assurance that anywhere he chose to go there were textiles. The difficulty lay in making a choice of what to study. Those choices were decided for him to some extent and his personal course of study redirected by the university's decision to phase out the design

22. **Printed Textile,** 1959 (detail)
Commercial cotton fabric, felt marker
Stencil resist dyed
112″ x 35 1/2″
Collection of the Artist

department during the late 60s and early 70s. Feeling an urgency to salvage the courses in textile history that threatened to be lost in the ensuing shuffle, Rossbach himself undertook to offer them. He thought it absolutely essential that the students have this background, so he expended a tremendous amount of energy in the preparation of course plans, researching, gathering slides and photographing objects in the Lowie Museum of Anthropology to add to the existing inadequate collection of slides available for the course. No one, he said, seemed to think much about his taking on the task, other than to suggest he might be spreading himself a little too thin. "But thin," he said, "was better than nothing—and at least I could give the students a sense of my enthusiasm."[29] A quick study, Rossbach adroitly translated his enthusiasm into painstakingly prepared courses, introducing a wealth of information on the techniques and materials of the world's textile traditions, and thereby influencing an untold number of students to invest new value in the subjects of their inquiries. (See Cook's discussion.)

The experience proved much more than an exercise in course preparation; the studies reverberated in Rossbach's creative output as well. He attributes his contacts with the Lowie's great collection of California Indian baskets with influencing the work he did at that time and his involvement with techniques and structure.

THE ENDURING CONTRIBUTIONS

It is Rossbach's involvement with the nature and history of basketmaking as a technique that perhaps has garnered him the most widespread critical acclaim and his unparalleled reputation in the contemporary fiber arts. Yet for all of the public accolades, his exploration of the basket is among his most spontaneous and personal work. His own baskets reveal most read-

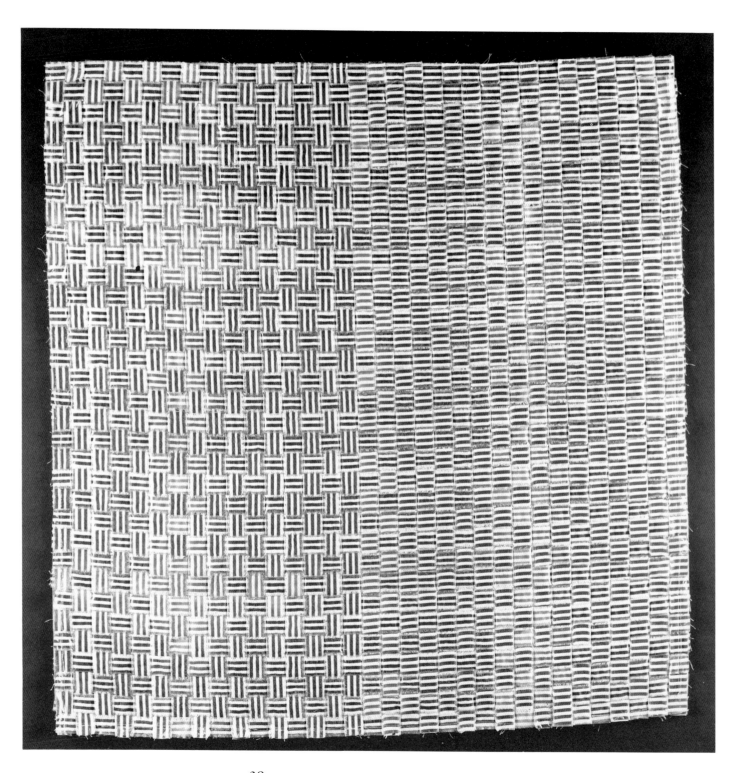

38

23. **Reconstituted Commercial Textile,** 1960
Polyethylene film tubing, commercial fabric with printed stripe
Tie-dyed and discharged, plaited
35 1/2″ x 35″
Collection of the Artist

24. **Raffia Panel,** 1964
Raffia
Plain weave with discontinuous warps and wefts interlocked
71″ x 45″
The Museum of Modern Art, New York
Greta Daniel Fund
Photo: The Museum of Modern Art

ily his gifts as an innovator and as a consummate craftsman; they bear witness to his command of traditional techniques and to his sometimes capricious departure from them. Acknowledging that although utility is no longer a consideration in basketmaking— at least in most Western cultures—Rossbach asserts that no artist is ever entirely dissociated from historical roots. Inevitably, these roots influence what a contemporary basketmaker does. "The *concept* of baskets throughout history is so tied to form and function, and specific cultures, that all this is somehow reflected in the new baskets, no matter how free from them the contemporary basketmaker seems, or perhaps would like to be. The idea of a basket exists somehow in the artist's mind, and that idea came from somewhere."[30]

Pondering the source of that idea is what lead Rossbach to write the second of his four published books.[31] *Baskets as Textile Art,* following *Making Marionettes,* which was published in his youth, appeared in 1973. It was first published in conjunction with the Museum of American Craft (now the American Craft Museum). Enlarged and updated with new illustrations and more color plates, it reappeared in 1986 retitled *The Nature of Basketry.* The initial publication was considered something of a coup, because at that time anything pertaining to craft that was not a "how to" book was a rarity. Its author was clearly uninterested in providing either instructions or struc-

25. **Wallhanging,** 1965
   Linen
   Double-cloth
   65" x 65"
   National Museum of American Art
   Smithsonian Institution
   Gift of the Artist

   Photo: National Museum of American Art

tural analysis; the book was instead a "personal interpretation, concerned with the aesthetic quality of baskets as it relates to process and material and human impulses,"[32] The success of *Baskets as Textile Art* led Rossbach to write *The New Basketry,* which was published in 1976 and focuses more on contemporary baskets created as a personal response to materials. His fourth book, *The Art of Paisley,* published in 1980, takes Rossbach in a decidedly different direction, although he is still intrigued with tracing an idea to its source. In this book he dwells on the home-based production of the paisley shawl prior to industrialization in 19th century Scotland. Another as yet unpublished study of 18th century French brocades and a staggering array of articles attest to his continuing fascination with a seemingly infinite variety of textile techniques. Rossbach sees the subjects of his scholarly inquiry and the writings which have resulted as inextricably related to his creative work and his teaching:

> Research has been central to all my work for thirty years. I hope no one asks me what research means because there is a wide spectrum of interpretation today. For me it was reading, reconstruction, experimentation to achieve the results I wanted. Some people don't want to be inhibited by what was done before they were born. They reject the past. They forget that technology builds on technology and art builds on art.[33]

The other creative outgrowths of Rossbach's fascination with process and technique—his artworks and his teaching—are considered at greater length in the other discussions included in this volume.

We have attempted in this discussion to provide a closer inspection of the foundation upon which Rossbach himself has built a career that is unparalleled in its prolific output. All of these circumstances come together to form this uniquely gifted individual, a

previous pages, from left:

26. **Hornets' Nest,** 1964
    Raffia, synthetic raffia, sisal, gesso
    Coiled
    9″ x 11 1/2″ x 11 1/2″
    Collection of the Artist

27. **Looped Cylinder,** 1964
    Rattan
    Looping
    13″ x 8 1/2″ x 7″
    Collection of the Artist

28. **Ceremonial Plate with Face,** 1965
    Ixtle
    Macrame
    14″ x 14″ x 3″
    Mr. and Mrs. Sanford M. Besser, Little Rock, Arkansas
    Photo: Vince Foster

genius in the field of fiber art. Rossbach has become an artist of eminence in his field whose life has been devoted to creativity and the pursuit of knowledge. This multi-faceted man has given the world beautiful potency and magic through his life's work. The germination and evolution of that work has enhanced the magnitude of fiber as an art form today and in the future.

29. **Basket with Handle,** 1966
    Wire frame, raffia
    Interlaced, wrapped
    11″ x 8″ x 8″
    American Craft Museum
    Gift of Johnson Wax Company, from *Objects: USA*

The artist's natural reticence and modesty would forbid his acknowledging the extent of his many contributions to the world of contemporary fiber art. This volume and the exhibition it accompanies, however, attempt to recognize and honor his enduring contributions. The self-appointed speaker for "no product," for the "satisfaction of just looking at something and it's gone," Ed Rossbach has left us a legacy in his life's work that will continue to educate and communicate long after the exhibition has come to a close and the book has taken its place on the shelf. Despite his many achievements and his deserving accolades, Rossbach, thinking of himself as "the last Puritan," expresses his inability to stop and his impatience to continue creating:

> I always had this enormous feeling that I had potentials which I have never explored . . . I suppose this is pure vanity . . . I had all sorts of intentions for doing good in education that I could never make use of. It isn't that you want to make money or that you want fame, not at all. The thing that comes through most teaching is the enormous capacities people have that are never explored.[34]

His humility, his humor, his patience, his diligence in discovering new techniques and materials, his reverence for the past and his vision for the future—all combine to communicate the compelling need to explore our own capacities for change and growth. In the process, he has taught us what it is to value that which is "value-less," to laugh at that which is unexpectedly and unabashedly delightful, to cultivate that which makes us curious, and to share with others that which sustains the spirit.

30. **Knit Reeds,** 1967
    Rattan, cotton string
    Elements shaped on template, assembled in tricot structure
    10 ″ x 12″ x 11″
    Collection of the Artist

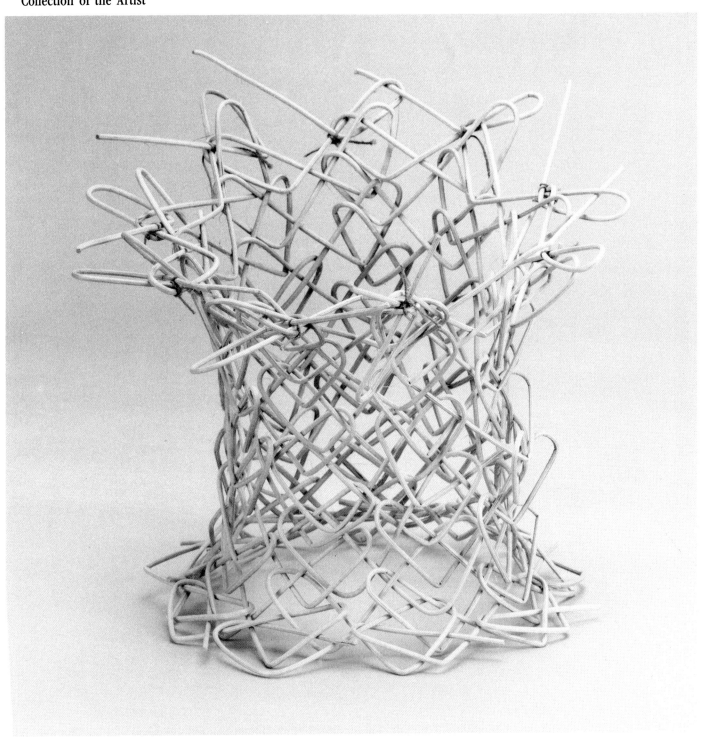

TEXTILE EXPLORATIONS
Ann Pollard Rowe

The variety of techniques available for interworking fibrous materials is truly staggering. Moreover, each requires some practice to master and each offers different aesthetic possibilities and limitations. In consequence, most fiber artists specialize. Ed Rossbach, however, has been fascinated by the potential of many different textile techniques, both those that require primarily hand manipulation and those that may have extensive mechanical control. This is not to say that he is interested in technique for its own sake; rather, he uses a given technique to achieve a result that could not be obtained in any other way.[1] In addition, he has explored a wide variety of materials, including those offered by contemporary urban life as well as the more traditional types of yarns. In doing so, he is concerned that the materials be appropriate for the structure and to the form, function and meaning of the piece.

Nothing in Rossbach's textile training at the Cranbrook Academy of Art suggested such an approach, although his ability to produce artistically interesting results within the confines of the limited forms taught was remarkable. Within the context of the Scandinavian Modern style taught at the school (see Corwin/Stevens discussion), weaving students were expected to produce prototypes for furnishing and suiting fabrics that could be industrially produced. Rossbach quotes his teacher, Marianne Strengell, as saying, "I want, above all, textures instead of pattern."[2] Cranbrook students wove only on a type of four-harness loom designed by Loja Saarinen which was based on Swedish contramarch looms, with warping and dressing the loom done in a particular way.

Students were not exposed to historical textiles. They made only rugs in tapestry (including with rag and rope wefts) and Scandinavian pile (flossa)[3] techniques and straight twill yardage. Students were not even allowed to reverse the direction of the twill diagonal to create herringbone! Twills were expected to have a mixed (striped) warp with only one or two different wefts so that the cloth could be woven quickly. A wand with holes in it was used to warp several colors simultaneously.

A plain-weave casement fabric of cotton and cellophane that Rossbach wove in 1946-47 has two wefts: a fine but slubby light colored one alternates with a wide even one.[4] The wide wefts bring out the slubbiness of the fine ones. The very fine spaced warps allow the wefts to dominate the fabric while their irregular spacing forms a counterpoint to the slubby wefts. The Cranbrook canon has not been violated here, and the structure is as simple as possible, but the effect is masterful. The use of cellophane is noteworthy in view of the extent to which Rossbach has used plastic in subsequent years. Some of his other fabrics of this period tended to use more wefts than the Cranbrook ideal, which gave him a little more scope (**Clothing Fabric** 1947, Fig. 2). Occasionally he broke out and improvised something totally outside the canon, as in a 1947 casement cloth with a Mondrian-like design, now in the Musee des Arts

31. At the damask drawloom at UC Berkeley, 1979.

Decoratifs de Montreal (accession number D85.164.1), which has knotted warps.

Rossbach entered fabrics in several of the annual International Textile Exhibitions sponsored by the art department of the Women's College of the University of North Carolina in Greensboro and won a number of prizes. In the 1947 show he won a first award in woven rugs for a tapestry cotton rag rug and another first for a woven linen.[5] The rag rug has a simple design of rectangles, with all the joins either at about a third of the way across or at the center. The linen is a plaid in natural, white and black, with the warp

stripes alternating light and dark closely but with interesting irregularities, creating a far from conventional effect.

He began to break out from the Cranbrook restrictions as soon as he left, but not until he began teaching at the University of California at Berkeley in 1950 did he have the stimulus and opportunity to study both different historical textile traditions and a wide variety of other textile techniques in depth. This exploration was stimulated by the nature of the weaving program at Berkeley, which was unique in the country at that time—and indeed there has never been another program anywhere else to equal it. Its basic features had been established by Lila Morris O'Neale (1886-1948) who had recently died.

O'Neale had studied and taught textiles in the Household Art Department at Berkeley and then had been suggested to analyze pre-Columbian Peruvian textiles for Alfred L. Kroeber, the distinguished professor of anthropology.[6] Subsequently she obtained her Ph.D. in anthropology at Berkeley under Kroeber, in 1930. Her dissertation, like that of all Kroeber's students, dealt with California Indians (in her case, Yurok-Karok baskets), and she also did important field work on Guatemalan textiles, but most of the rest of her publications describe pre-Columbian Peruvian textiles.[7] O'Neale's forte was description of the different structures found in these textiles, and she especially liked to try to reconstruct the way in which an archaeological textile might have been woven, as for example she did with Peruvian twills and gauze weaves.[8]

Her interests were reflected in the course of study offered in the Decorative Art Department. There were historical courses with lab sections in which the students learned the techniques. Anthropological textiles were brought to class for first hand study. In addition, exhibit cases in the hall displayed pieces from the Museum of Anthropology collection and the students were required to identify the techniques used to produce these pieces. O'Neale's successor, Anna Hadwick Gayton (1899-1977, taught 1948-1965), also received her Ph.D. in anthropology under Kroeber, in 1928. Unlike O'Neale, however, she did not have a textile background, her previous work having been in pottery analysis and folklore.[9] Thus she had to learn as she went along, a challenge she capably met, and she initially continued O'Neale's program, which was in place when Rossbach came to Berkeley.

In order to keep ahead of the students, Rossbach had to learn the techniques as well. He felt it was not possible to understand the techniques by reading alone but considered it necessary to try them out and also to make a finished piece, sometimes one, sometimes more.[10] He wanted to understand not only how to execute each technique but also to understand the properties and possibilities unique to each. He was interested as well in investigating how the techniques were used historically and how they might have meaning for our own time.

This approach is an artistic one and Rossbach from the beginning of his career never doubted that he was producing art. In a 1948 article on the rugs of Edna Vogel, Signe Ortiz and Robert Sailors, entitled "Handweaving as an Art Form," Rossbach states plainly his view of weaving which foreshadows the entire subsequent fiber art movement:

32. **Golden Ikat,** 1970
Silk
Plain weave, warp ikat
103" x 35"
Collection of the Artist

33. **Cellophane Ikat,** 1964
Cellophane
Plain weave, warp ikat
107" x 41 1/2"
Collection of the Artist

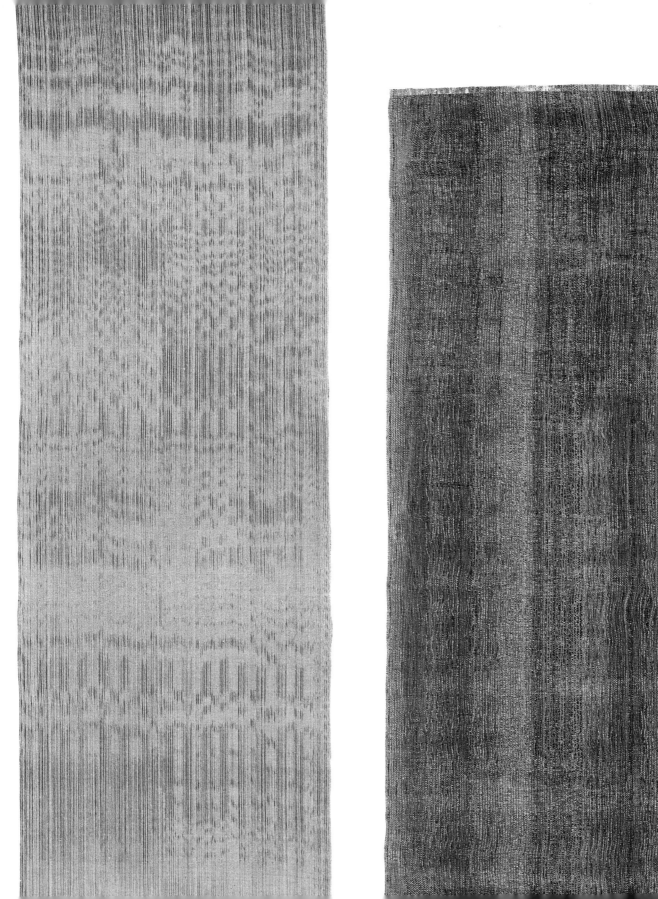

Today a Gothic Tapestry, a Finnish coverlet or a Peruvian garment may momentarily convince us that hand-weaving is indeed a lost art. We may despair to see the craft practiced only half-heartedly, with an eye to the commercial market and the easy effect which enable hand-weavers to compete with power-looms.

Yet occasionally we are heartened by discovery of contemporary weavers using the medium sensitively and creatively, aware that weaving is as expressive an art form as painting, sculpture, pottery or architecture.

The most daring and original use of pattern, color and texture in weaving today is found in rugs which no matter how small, are self-contained units, unlike draperies or clothing fabrics, with beginnings and endings, with composition and relationships as complex as those in any other work of art.[11]

Of course Rossbach's screens, wall hangings, baskets, sculptures and even some of the three-yard exhibition lengths also are self-contained units with composition and the other artistic qualities mentioned. Although Rossbach obviously considers it possible for a utilitarian textile to be art (and I certainly agree), in fact most of his pieces have a primarily aesthetic rather than utilitarian purpose. He had extensive art training and he has approached all of his work from this perspective. Fortunately he has had the inner strength not to allow anyone else's doubts about the validity of textiles as art to discourage him from working in his chosen way.[12]

Although the following text attempts to be approximately chronological, it also groups the pieces that are made in similar techniques in order to clarify the discussion. It should be remembered, however, that grouping things in this way does not reflect Rossbach's actual working method, since he is often involved with several different techniques simultaneously, to an even greater extent than is ap-

parent by comparing the dates of the pieces selected for illustration in this volume. Nevertheless, he does tend to work in series: frequently the process of making one piece will give him an idea for the next. In a 1971 tribute to Jack Lenor Larsen, he notes, "When things are going well, every textile that an artist produces increases—in geometric progression—the number of textiles he feels compelled to produce."[13] Rossbach works spontaneously, making artistic decisions as the piece takes shape, not doing any elaborate preplanning or mock-ups. He does do sketching, which may or may not lead to a finished work.

UPHOLSTERY AND CASEMENT FABRICS

During the 1950s he continued to work within the nominally utilitarian forms of the Cranbrook tradition such as casements and upholstery fabrics in the standard three-yard "exhibition" lengths, as well as rugs and screens, although he made no effort to market these fabrics to industry.

His 1949 **Double-cloth Fabric** (Fig. 1) is woven in a technique not taught at Cranbrook. Here he has used it, not in the usual way, which is to make a two-color design in a balanced weave, but to explore its potential for color mixing. Each stripe has four colors of warp, all of which are visible in the wider section woven in one layer but interrupted at intervals by narrow bands in which two of the colors are excluded. In the lower double-layer part, two of these colors appear on each face. Because there are fewer warps in each layer they are not quite so closely spaced and a contrasting color of weft shows through in shiny specks of color, in some stripes green and in others pink.

Upholstery Fabric, 1959 (Fig. 15), is in twill weave, but in some of the narrow warp stripes larger, darker warps make the twill diagonal more prominent than in the rest of the fabric. In other wider stripes, every fourth warp is wider and darker than the intervening ones, which in a 2/2 twill forms dark warp floats in horizontal alignment.[14] In the weft there are also some narrow stripes of white slubby wefts. These devices add complexity to the basic plaid.

His use of gauze weave in casements was influenced by Lea Miller, a colleague in the Decorative Art Department at Berkeley, who in turn had been inspired by O'Neale's work in this subject. Both the casements shown here use this structure. **Casement**, 1951 (Fig. 6), also employs plastic ribbon which was given to him by Miller.[15] However, he felt this was Miller's territory and did not pursue the idea of weaving gauze with plastic further. In **Casement Cloth**, 1952 (Fig. 10), the verticality of the gauze structure is emphasized by using warp stripes to set off the smooth heavy yarns that cross each other, but rigidity is avoided by using an overspun weft and boucle warps between the gauze pairs.[16]

RUGS AND SCREENS

Unfortunately, few of Rossbach's rugs seem to have survived. The 1952 **Rug** shown here (Fig. 11) is woven with supplementary wefts in three-span floats in a draft commonly known as "summer and winter," which he learned from a draft of Mary Atwater's on file in the Decorative Art Department at Berkeley.[17] Traditional coverlets woven with such drafts have block patterns similar to other types of 19th century North American coverlets woven on four-harness looms. Rossbach instead made a banded pattern, repeating but not symmetrical.

Although Rossbach credits casements and rugs as the chief forms from which the new wall hangings evolved in the late 1950s,[18] screens seem to have been more important in the development of Rossbach's own work. He was inspired by Dorothy Liebes' use of wooden slats and other rigid elements as wefts in blinds and screens.[19] This idea was important for stimulating the imaginative use of materials, which Rossbach has pursued throughout his career.[20] In addition, screens possess a scale that highlights their structural organization, another concern of Rossbach in his later work.

Although most weavers made screens only in plain weave, Rossbach observed that most imported (from the Far East) and commercial blinds were held together with warp twining, which enabled the wefts to be held securely with a minimum number of warps. He employed both warp twining and gauze in addition to plain weave in his screens.[21] In **African Reeds**, 1952 (Fig. 12), the warp twining of linen holds the flexible wefts (inserted after every second reed) so firmly that they actually curve as they pass over the paper.[22] The strips of gold and silver metallic paper are inserted in a checkerboard pattern, parallel to the warp, so that the entire surface is light reflective.

Another (untitled) piece that illustrates how creative Rossbach could be in this medium is pictured in Constantine and Larsen's *Beyond Craft*.[23] Spaced gauze warps and stiff anise stalk wefts form a grid which is filled in with raffia wefts alternating dark and light to create a checked effect. However, the spacing of the grid is varied, and the color changes often have an intermeshed effect instead of a straight vertical, giving the piece a much greater surface interest.

following page:

34. **Constructed Color,** 1965
Synthetic yarn, raffia
Braided
57" x 71"
The Museum of Modern Art, New York
Purchase
Photo: The Museum of Modern Art

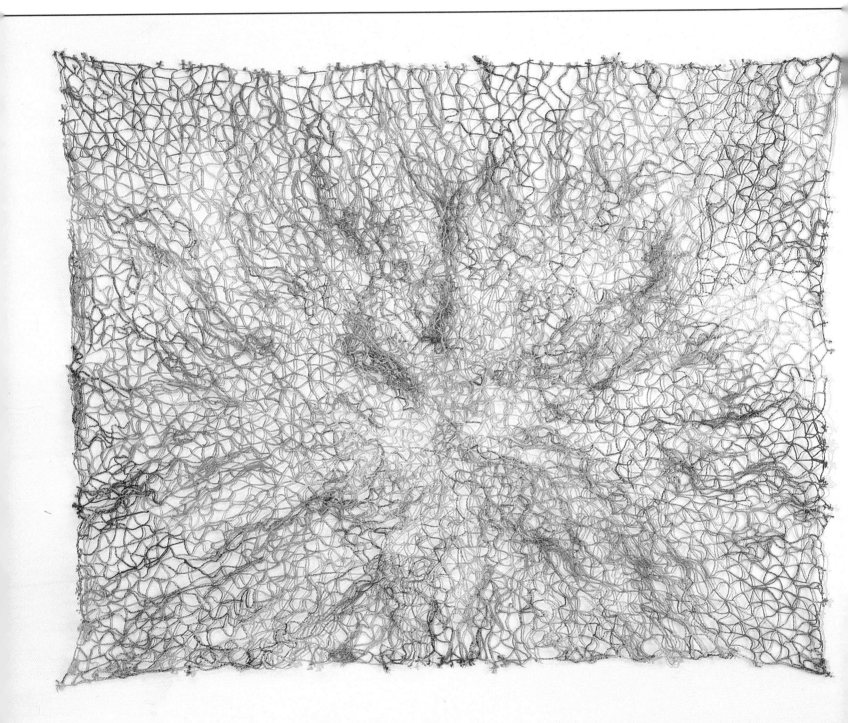

Tule Screen, 1954 (Fig. 7), is in plain weave, but with asymmetry in the warps. Rossbach uses flexible wefts alternately with the rigid ones to prevent the warps from moving outward toward the edges. The flexible wefts form a pattern of their own since each weft only passes about two thirds of the way across the fabric, alternately from each selvedge, and are in alternating colors, yellow and pink from one side and yellow and blue from the other. Thus the central part of the screen where the warps are in narrower units has a bit more color than the sides. The screen is made with tules he gathered himself from the Sacramento delta, inspired by the use of tules in California Indian mats.[24] The material is soft and spongy and squashes down slightly on the loom.

RAFFIA WEAVING

African Congo Weaving I and **II**, 1952 (Fig. 4-5), were explorations of the possibilities in the loom weaving of raffia, a fiber of limited length which cannot be spun, and they make no pretense of being utilitarian. Rossbach says of them:

> At the time I wove these, shortly after I came to teach at Berkeley, I was preoccupied with thoughts about looms. Berkeley gave me my first contact with primitive looms, and aroused questions about distinctions between darning and weaving, and about exactly what features were required to make something a loom rather than merely a frame. I was interested in precise definitions. The Ciba Reviews on anthropological subjects were a great source of enlightenment. The Department in which I was teaching had a textile collection that included a Congo raffia weaving which, from the beginning, was one of my favorite textiles.
>
> My first raffia panel was an attempt to weave raffia on a European-type loom. I encountered very many problems which suggested to me that my loom was inappropriate for the materials I was using. In the second panel I tried to solve some of the problems by shredding the raffia as the Congo raffia weavers did, and by spacing the strands farther apart in the warp, and by keeping the area to be woven free of knots. I had been unable to weave the first panel in plain weave because the strands were too close together; I had to resort to a twill which was not what I wanted. Even then the wefts wouldn't pack in as I had expected. I was hoping for a very simple declaration of weaving with un-spun elements. Despite the numerous difficulties, I was pleased with the results— more pleased than anyone else has been. I don't think my fondness can be attributed to the amount of trouble they were to weave. But who can say?[25]

Raffia was a common material in the crafts at that time and Rossbach used it in other kinds of pieces also, as will be noted below. The African technique of weaving it is to make plain-weave cloth on a simple vertical loom; some examples are patterned with supplementary wefts.[26] Because of the limited length of the fiber, the warp length is sometimes extended by tying the ends to cords that are not part of the

following pages, from left:

35. **San Blas**, 1967
    Cotton, linen
    Plain weave with discontinuous warps and wefts interlocked, weft twining
    67" x 66"
    Collection of the Artist

36. **Kalahari**, 1966 - 1967
    Jute
    Gauze weave, discontinuous warps, weft twining
    67 1/2" x 51 1/2"
    Collection of the Artist

53

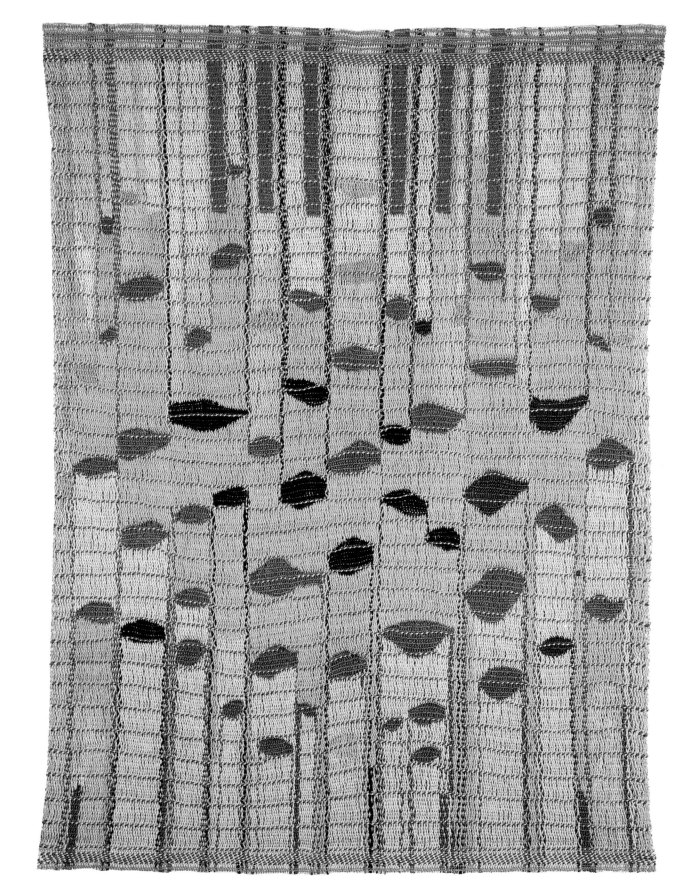

finished fabric. The wefts customarily extend beyond the edges of the warps to form a fringe.

Although Rossbach was weaving his pieces on a European style treadle loom, he employed the same devices of tying the ends of the warp to separate elements which went through the heddles so as to be able to weave the entire length, and in addition he allowed the wefts to extend beyond the side selvedges. The limited length of the fiber dictated the unusual size of these pieces. In **African Congo Weaving I**, the twill direction, visible in the warp floats, changes with increasing (or decreasing) frequency across the piece, although this effect is subtle since the elements are relatively uniform in color. In the second example, the changes in the direction of the twill correlate approximately with the placement of the warp stripes. The dark weft stripes draw attention to the peaks in the twill.

IKAT

Rossbach became very interested in ikat (resist dyeing of yarns before weaving) during the 1950s, which was most unusual among fiber artists of that period. Its appeal goes back even to his work at Cranbrook when he painted on a warp, to the dismay of his teachers.[27] However, he was further stimulated to explore this technique by the anthropologically oriented course given at Berkeley. He found that he could use imagery that he had not been able to use before: the idea of discontinuous color. He enjoyed as well the varied challenges this technique presented.[28] For example, he did a piece with spiral patterns, and he also attempted to replicate a technique from India that someone had described to him where the warps to be tied were wound extended out on spokes on a sort of wheel. He eventually decided that this technique must have made it possible to wind each warp over one of several radiating pegs and to tie the warps on different spokes

in a different way, which scattered the design.

His first pieces are in warp ikat, woven in the then standard three-yard exhibition lengths. However, they are not necessarily yardage; many have non-repeating patterns, as for example **Double Ikat**, 1956 (Fig. 14).[29] He had less and less concern with utility as time went on. He started producing ikats with discharge (bleaching previously dyed yarns) rather than direct dyeing because he found this method easier to control. Then Lea Miller taught him the use of Ciba dyes. He was not interested in the dyeing process itself and never experimented with natural dyes.

In some of Rossbach's ikats the pattern occurs in spaced warp stripes with solid stripes between so that there is an interesting interplay between the colors of the ikat and the plain stripes. In the striped **Ikat**, 1956 (Fig. 13), the white reserved areas form new shapes with adjacent white stripes. In addition, the warp stripes were tied at different intervals.[30] The idea came from a ballet he had seen in which the dancers each moved across the stage at a different pace, some slower and some faster. He began to see the ikats also as measuring time or space.[31]

Some of the warp ikats have subtle weft stripes.[32] Some are woven in twill rather than plain weave, which adds diagonal lines to whatever verticals and horizontals might be created by stripes, as in the 1956 **Double Ikat** (Fig. 14). As with weft stripes, these diagonals pass through the dyed areas and can unify or break up the dyed pattern depending on the spacing of the yarns and the type of twill used. In **Double Ikat**, a balanced twill in a balanced spacing tends to make the ikat appear even more diffuse and helps to blend the dyed patterns of the warps and wefts.

Thus, although traditional ikats usually aim for precise delineation of design areas despite the difficulty of attaining it with this technique, Rossbach more often sought to create diffuse color areas. Similarly, when he combined warp and weft ikat he wanted it to be

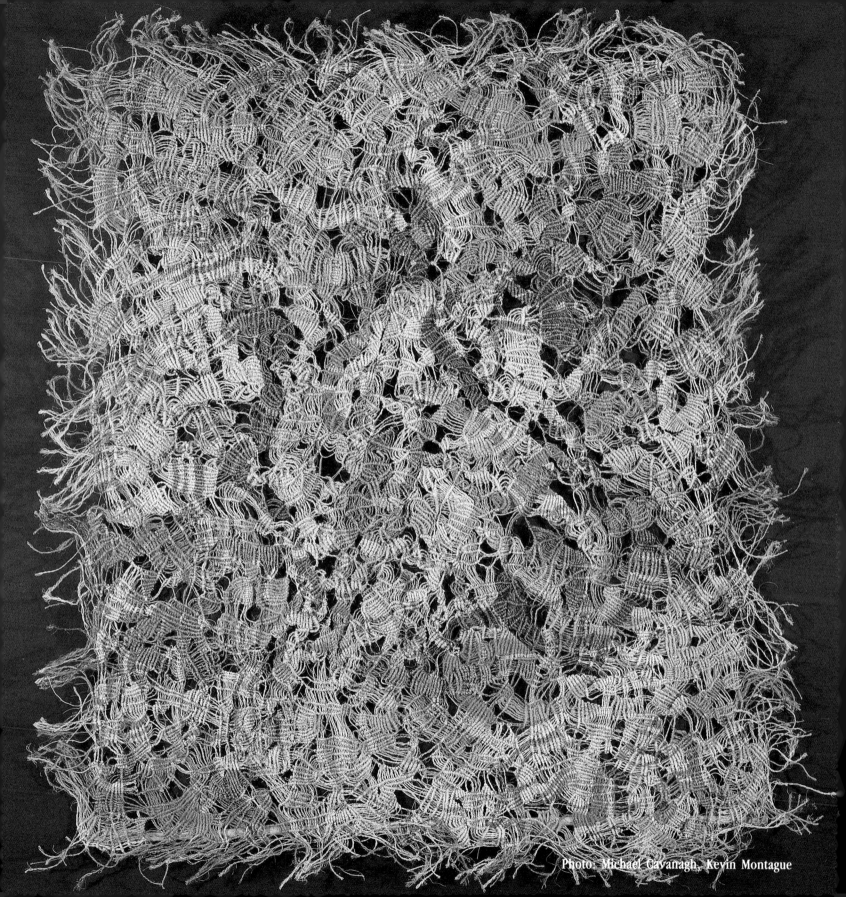

random, the way it is in Guatemalan ikats. He commented that Ann Gayton did not like this randomness, so he did it almost defiantly.

Golden Ikat, 1970 (Fig. 32), has very narrow but irregularly sized warp stripes, ikat-dyed purple alternating with solid yellow, crossed by a reddish weft, all of which serves to disperse the pattern.[33] A similar effect is found in **Cellophane Ikat**, 1964 (Fig. 33), with narrow ikat (flat cellophane) and solid color (two strips of cellophane twisted together) stripes, but in this case the shimmer of the cellophane diffuses the pattern still more.[34] The weft is a clear cellophane so that it does not register as part of the design at all.

A number of the ikats were made by first putting the warp on the loom and inserting a fine temporary weft, widely spaced. The idea came from his reading about the chine silks of the 18th and 19th centuries in France and England.[35] Then this fabric was tie-dyed by tying small rocks into the cloth, the temporary weft was removed and the final weft woven in. In traditional ikat, groups of warps are tied together, so Rossbach's technique prevents the blockiness that would ordinarily result. He also sometimes used this technique of temporary wefts when he wanted to stencil, paint, or otherwise print the warps.[36] He liked the color mixing that occurred with an undyed weft and the fact that the edges of the designs blurred.

One of Rossbach's textiles with painted warp was adapted by Jack Lenor Larsen and called **Bamako.**[37] The original textile (1960, Fig. 19) has the warps painted in a strong blue in a design inspired by the medallions used to decorate classical Greek vases; red and blue weft stripes, woven in plain weave, appear in a superficially regular arrangement, but are actually not quite regular. Larsen's adaptation (1962-63, Fig. 18) has the Greek design silkscreened onto the warp, making the design appear more subtle. Its colors are also significantly more muted. To obtain the mottled effect of the weft stripes, Larsen had it woven in a

warp-predominant 2/1 twill, and turned the weave in some of the stripes. The weft color is thus stronger when the weft-float face is visible and more mottled when the warp-float face is visible.

Although Rossbach's **Homage to Japan**, 1970 (Fig. 51), is a later piece, made as a wall hanging and not as a single three-yard length, it illustrates the techniques described above and is perhaps the culmination of his investigation of ikat.[38] He wove the two parts as one length, carefully planning the design to match when it was cut and seamed. The warp was tie dyed while woven with a temporary weft. After weaving the temporary weft, he took the warp out of the reed but left it still tied on the loom. Then he folded it in half and tie-dyed it using small rocks. The ties were put through the weaving, somewhat like stitch resist, not just tied around it. The warp design has recognizably tie-dyed diamonds in some areas and elsewhere dissolves into more nebulous forms. The weft ikat forms large cross shapes, reinforcing the warp design at one end and contradicting it at the other.

Having explored double ikat, he began to experiment more with weft ikat alone. He felt that doing a picture with weft ikat (the Japanese ekasuri technique) was almost magical. However, this technique is easier to control if the piece is small, so he did not explore it fully until after he had stopped weaving three-yard lengths. In this technique, the orientation of the design depends on what side of the warp the weft is first inserted and also on which end of the weft is used first. Rossbach liked to combine the different orientations on one piece, as for example in **Kasuri Heads III**, 1966 (Fig. 21), where the upper right and lower left faces are the same (but reversed), as are the upper left and lower right.[39] He also made a piece with two ikatted wefts alternating so that the patterns overlap.

Inspired by the idea of changing the design orientation, he also tried it in some of his pieces with woven

previous pages:

38. **Construction with Newspaper and Plastic,** 1968
    Polyethylene film tubing, polyethylene twine,
       newspaper
    Plain weave
    30″ x 40″
    The Museum of Modern Art, New York
    Gift of the Designer
    Photo: The Museum of Modern Art

40. **Early Cross,** 1967
    Wool, cotton
    Knotted netting with pile
    13″ x 13″
    Collection of the Artist

39. **Young Hercules,** 1967
    Jute, cotton, ixtle
    Looping
    80″ x 41″
    Collection of the Artist

61

patterns, as in **Log Cabin Sham**, 1967 (Fig. 44), where vertically and horizontally oriented units alternate.[40] He also tried turning the design in double cloth at about the same time. Although natural to weft ikat, the changes in the weaving designs had to be done with pickup. In **Log Cabin Sham**, the overall design is based on log cabin quilts, but each rectangle is woven with a different overshot (supplementary weft) pattern which means that the treadling had to be changed for each one. Rossbach wove the first pattern repeat himself and then had an assistant finish the weaving. She did well but this was the only time he ever used assistance. His sense of removal from the process and the resulting aversion to using assistants explains why he has done comparatively few large pieces.

A different use of ikat is found in **Modular Construction**, 1968 (Fig. 46), which is woven in tapestry technique (the piece is hung with the warp horizontal). The striped squares are made with a single ikatted weft in which the color changes at the point where the weft is turned. The piece was made in two panels, one of which was cut in half after weaving and sewn to each side of the other panel. The narrow end panels are also separately made. The quieter ends frame but do not totally contain the more active central section. The tapestry joins are accentuated by the use of narrow areas of coarser yarn perpendicular to the stripes. Rossbach has said that this was one of his favorite pieces.

SURFACE DESIGN

Throughout his career, Rossbach has been involved with surface design, although his textiles in this medium are less well known than his other work. He has used block prints, silk screen, paste and wax resists, drawing and painting, heat transfers (from color photocopy), and tie dye, sometimes separately but more often in combination.[41] He has also felt free to combine designs from different sources in the same piece. For his printed textiles he has used mainly Inko dyes and Prang Textile Colors.

Stencilled Textile, 1953 (Fig. 16), has a simple design closer to the Scandinavian Modern of his schooling than does his other surface design work. The unbroken color areas permit the texture of the Mexican handwoven fabric to assert itself. The strong colors are appropriate for Mexican cloth. Rossbach said this piece was inspired by a Mimbres pot with a "kill" hole in the bottom.[42]

Most of Rossbach's other surface design work is more expressionistic in character, exploiting varied colors, textures, and designs. In his review of a surface design show in 1978 he admits his enjoyment of repeating patterns.[43] In **Wood Block and Resist**, 1960 (Fig. 20), he used small wood blocks he made himself, between 2″ and 6″ long. After printing with the blocks, he did batik over these designs. **Printed Textile**, 1959 (Fig. 22), has many layers of stencilling with paste resist and dyeing. The layering provides a dense and detailed patterning. This piece gives the superficial impression of repeating patterns, and indeed the small elements repeat, but the arrangement is variable.

He did not pursue this medium during the 1960s. When he began again, he used larger scale patterns without repeats. **Ground Cloth**, 1972 (Fig. 52), was done using stencils and paste resist (made by Inko). The superposition of the large color areas on the small dotted patterns gives a dramatic effect. The title refers to the type of cloth one spreads out on the ground for a picnic.

Sketch for a Vestment, 1978 (Fig. 94), **Toftner Square**, 1980 (Fig. 76), and **Sports Illustrated**, 1980 (Fig. 93), are silk screened but with additions in heat transfer and, in the case of the first two, drawing with felt pen. The principal inspiration for **Sketch for**

a **Vestment** is from a fragmentary vestment of French brocaded silk in the Design Department collection, from which it was nevertheless possible to reconstruct the whole repeat. This design is silk screened in red in the center of the piece, while over it is a point paper pattern for a Paisley shawl (the green areas of which came out lace-like). The diagonals at the sides and centers are denser heat transfers from photocopies of Chinese ribbons. Lines in black felt pen run down the center. These disparate elements are unified by the arrangement of color and the large oblong shapes in the center.

Rossbach studied both French silks and Paisley shawls extensively enough to produce books on these subjects, although unfortunately the former has not yet found a publisher. It is appropriate that he has used drawings of such designs, especially the point paper patterns of Paisley shawls, for a graphic medium like silk screen rather than trying to give a more literal interpretation of the original fabric. He says of these pieces, "I want fragments of images and fragments of techniques, old and new, scattered and superimposed."[44]

WALL HANGINGS

After about 1960 Rossbach ceased to make yardage or other fabrics that could be construed as utilitarian. He turned instead to making wall hangings, baskets, and small sculptures. He was not one of the leaders in promoting the idea of wall hangings, the first glimmerings of which appeared in an exhibition at the Museum of Modern Art in 1956,[45] but by the mid-1960s this was his major production. Wall hangings certainly allow the same advantages for artistic expression that he had noted for rugs in 1948. One such piece executed relatively early is his **Wallhanging**, 1965 (Fig. 25), in double cloth, now in the National Museum of American Art's Renwick Gallery collection, which was first exhibited early in 1966.[46] It was woven in nar-

row bands on a table loom.

These looms were in use in the department at Berkeley and Rossbach had used them earlier as well. In an article published in 1950 he notes, "A designer for the floor loom achieves his effects through varied warp, simple weft, and simple treadling pattern, whereas the designer for the table loom simplifies his warp in favor of a complicated weft and treadling pattern."[47] This succinctly expresses the different advantages of these two types of looms. The technique of double cloth, which requires pickup to create the design, is advantageously woven on a table loom.

The designs in **Wallhanging** are all used in both their negative and positive versions, taking advantage of the possibility of exact reversals offered by the fabric structure and creating an optically active effect. Straight-sided designs alternate irregularly with a net-like one in various sizes. The vertical design changes as often as the horizontal. While many of the patterns fill the full width of the band, others change down the middle and there are also variations in the widths of the bands. Thus the horizontal changes are no more regular than the vertical ones. Although the black and white are regularly exchanged, there is a

following pages, from left:

41. **Layered Mesh,** 1970
Polyethylene garbage bags
Looping
35" x 39"
Collection of the Artist

42. **Tubular Construction,** 1969
Polyethylene film tubing, rayon, cotton
Plaited, knotted
40" x 34"
Milwaukee Art Museum
Gift of Floyd and Dorothy Segel
Photo: Richard Eells

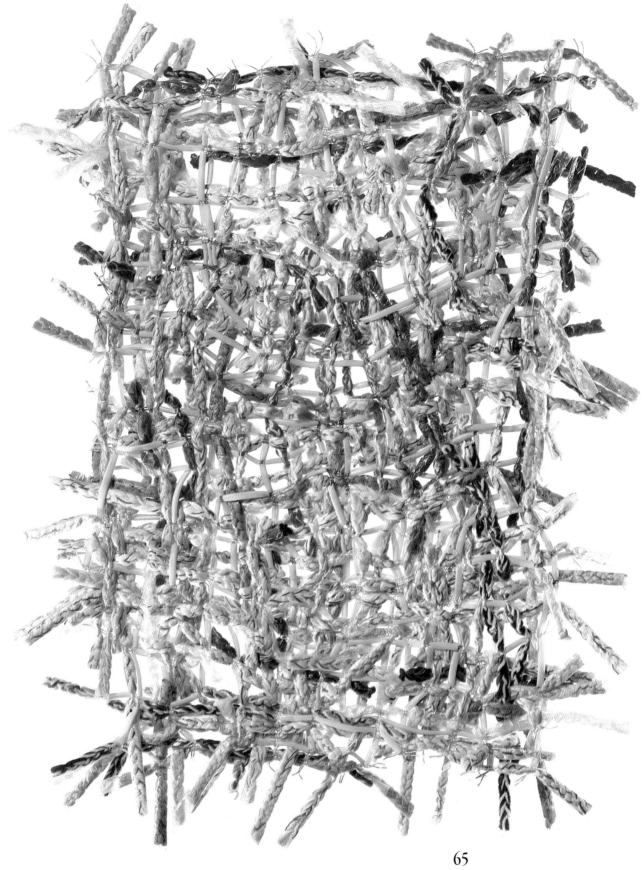

65

slight weighting toward the black on the side with the blue border and toward white on the side with the red border. These side borders ultimately contain and unify the composition.

FOUR-SELVEDGE INTERLACING

Rossbach also explored the structure of discontinuous warp and weft during the 1960s. Use of this structure again was unusual among fiber artists, but an outgrowth of his study of anthropological textiles, in this case those of pre-Spanish Peru. In Peru, the structure is the ultimate development of the idea of weaving fabrics with four selvedges, which is characteristic of most textiles woven in pre-Spanish America (and by many native Americans today). To create such fabrics, the warp is bound to the loom bars without being cut and the heddle cord is wrapped around the warps. This type of setup is used whether the loom is backstrap, staked out, or secured to a vertical or other frame. Fabrics with discontinuous warps were also set up on an apparatus like a loom, with adjustable tension; the evidence suggests that the Peruvians warped these textiles over scaffold rods for which a weft was later substituted.[48] Nevertheless, the detailed procedures are unknown. If the design areas were large enough, heddles were used to aid in weft insertion; in many instances, however, the designs are so small that the wefts would have had to be darned in with a needle, as is done for the final wefts in any four-selvedge textile.

Rossbach was interested in the structural effect of this technique (discontinuous color, as in ikats), rather than in the technique itself, which in any case is not fully understood. Thus he invented a variety of techniques to achieve a similar structure, using a rigid frame instead of a loom. In consequence, he also expanded the vocabulary of visual possibilities.

His best known work in this structure, and deservedly so, is **Raffia Panel**, 1964 (Fig. 24), in the collection of The Museum of Modern Art.[49] It was done on an open frame, with a multitude of tacks around the edge. He established a narrow warp the full length of the frame and wove it. Next he established a warp perpendicular to the first, extending from the center of the side edge of the first warp to the edge of the frame, and wove that. He then made a warp parallel to the second on the opposite side of the first one, etc. It was a matter of balancing the tension of each warp against the preceding ones in order to create a flat plane. If this method seems related to paintings and theories of Mondrian, whose stated goal was to establish an equilibrium "through the balance of unequal but equivalent oppositions," such a thought was also in Rossbach's mind.[50] When the piece was finished, the frame had warped, so Rossbach cut it off the frame, at which point it became a flexible panel. The Museum of Modern Art remounted it, recreating the effect of the frame on which it had been made.

One can see that the first vertical warp and the major horizontal ones that branch out from it have been pulled slightly out of alignment by the subsequent weaving, a refinement that does not occur in the Peruvian pieces which had only warp-wise tension. The grid-like design follows naturally from the technique but with enough variation to avoid monotony. A striking feature of this panel is that it is monochrome, or nearly so. In the Peruvian pieces that inspired Rossbach, the purpose of changing the warp was to change the color, but Rossbach focuses instead on the change in texture made by the joining of warps and wefts and on the change in density from one area to another made possible by the use of separately made warps.

In **Kalahari**, 1966-67 (Fig. 36), he has produced a striking piece which approaches the structure of discontinuous warps in a manner quite different from **Raffia Panel** as well as from Peruvian examples. In

43. **World Egg,** 1969
    Sisal, jute, polyethylene
       film tubing
    Macrame
    25 1/2″ x 28 1/2″
    Collection of the Artist
    Photo: the Artist

44. **Log Cabin Sham,** 1967
    (detail)
    Cotton, linen
    Overshot Weave (plain weawith supplementary weft
       interlocked)
    60 1/2″ x 23 3/4″
    Collection of the Artist

45. **Vinyl Log Cabin,** 1970
    Vinyl flagging tape
    Heat bonded
    77″ x 56″
    Collection of the Artist

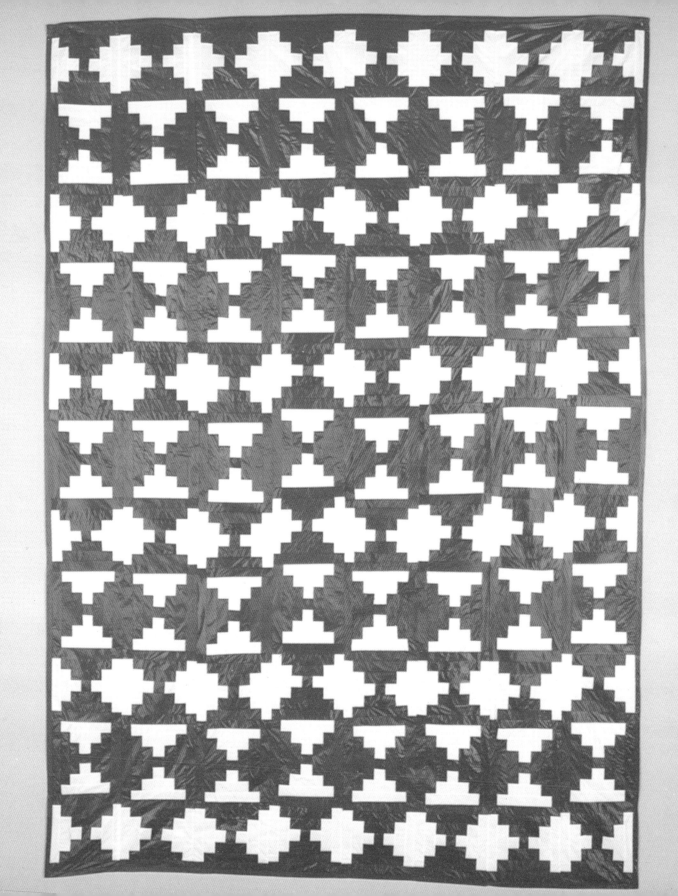

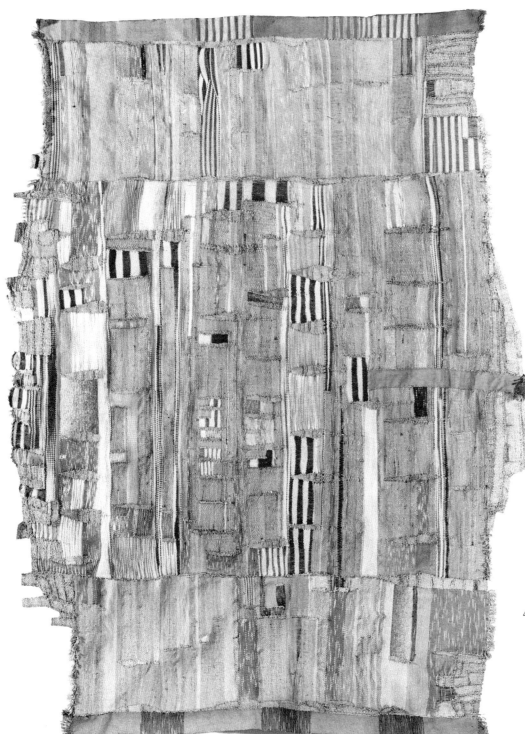

46. **Modular Construction,** 1968
Cotton, linen, silk, raffia
Interlocked tapestry weave,
    weft ikat, cut and sewn
64 3/4″ x 48″
Milwaukee Art Museum
Gift of Karen Johnson Boyd
Photo: Richard Eells

this case, he prepared the warp by pinning it down on a Celotex board. The warps predominate (with interlocked joins) and are woven in simple alternating gauze with one non-holding weft after each gauze weft, which emphasizes the glossiness of the jute yarns.[51] He has set up a subtle grid by various means. He uses narrow stripes of dark warps (which cross yellow ones) and twined wefts (dark and yellow twisted together) at similar intervals. The twining also helped stabilize the piece as it was being made. Both ends are beautifully finished with extra rows of twining. The wefts are continuous, changing color after each twined row, from orange to grey or vice versa. Since the piece is warp-predominant, this striping is very subtle.

The warps in **San Blas**, 1967 (Fig. 35), were also pinned to a Celotex board, but in this case a greater variety of forms was used, including curvilinear ones, a feature rarely attempted by the Peruvians. The wefts may pass through several color areas or may change in the middle of a warp color area, devices again not found in Peruvian textiles, but adding a layering effect inspired by San Blas applique molas. The color mixing is reminiscent of his ikats. The strong colors are also due to mola influence. Occasional rows of twining again stabilize the interlacing, cutting through the designs in a manner similar to the rest of the wefts. This piece was of course extremely time consuming to make, and Rossbach left the edges unfinished.

Rossbach also used the technique of interlacing on a frame to create four selvedge pieces with continuous warps and wefts. In this case, the frame was a way of working with extra large elements. He was interested in large elements because he wanted the structure to be plainly visible, as it is in technical diagrams in books, which he found so appealing in themselves.[52] In a piece like **Construction with Newspaper and Plastic**, 1968 (Fig. 38), the visual interest lies not in the structure, which is plain interlacing, but in the

materials used to create the large elements.[53] The technique does provide a clean finished edge which otherwise would have been problematic to achieve with these materials.

Rossbach says he used stuffed plastic tubing as a way to get extra large elements. But more than this, Rossbach simply likes the material. He says, "I could stretch plastic over everything and it looks wonderful."[54] When something has plastic over it, it looks shiny and new. The tubing was a packaging material bought in rolls, not particularly easy to get.

The ready availability of newspaper in our urban environment was, on the other hand, a significant factor in its appeal. But again, Rossbach just happens to like it, the texture, the sense of the ordinariness of it. He says about one of his newspaper baskets, "I was not remotely interested in seeming clever or in making a statement about newspapers in our society, yet when the baskets were finished the letters and words and fragments of illustrations added a peculiar force. They seem to speak out with an undeniable message. Sometimes I am reminded that the Indians thought their baskets contained the spirit that resided in the vegetation."[55]

Encasing the newspaper in plastic, as he often does, tends to preserve it to some extent. However, Rossbach also does not mind the evanescence of some of his materials. He says, "I like doing things that I think could possibly last and things that obviously aren't going to last too long."[56] He also notes, "Built-in obsolescence is a familiar concept which we are coming to accept in what we consider to be our non-art utilitarian objects . . . Increasingly our art is not concerned with posterity. The validity of everything is in the 'now.' The idea of art that is evanescent or self-destructible becomes more and more intriguing. We enshrine for the moment the found object of no intrinsic value."[57] **Construction with Newspaper and Plastic** embodies all these ideas. The simple four sel-

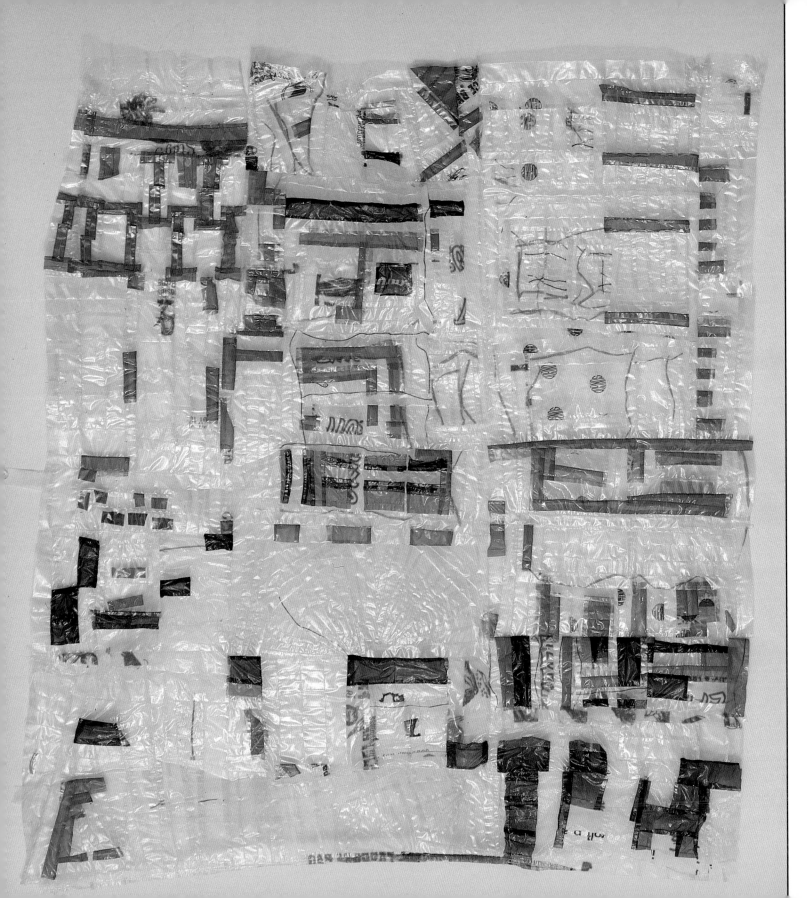

47. Slip Cover for a Computer,
 1969
Polyethylene film commercial
 food wrappers, polyethy-
 lene film
Heat bonded
36″ x 31 3/4″
The Museum of Modern Art,
 New York
NEA Architecture and Design
 Fund and Purchase
Photo: The Museum of
 Modern Art

48. Jet X10, 1971
Polyethylene film tubing,
 styrofoam, found objects
Plaited, heat bonded
54″ x 35 1/2″
Collection of the Artist

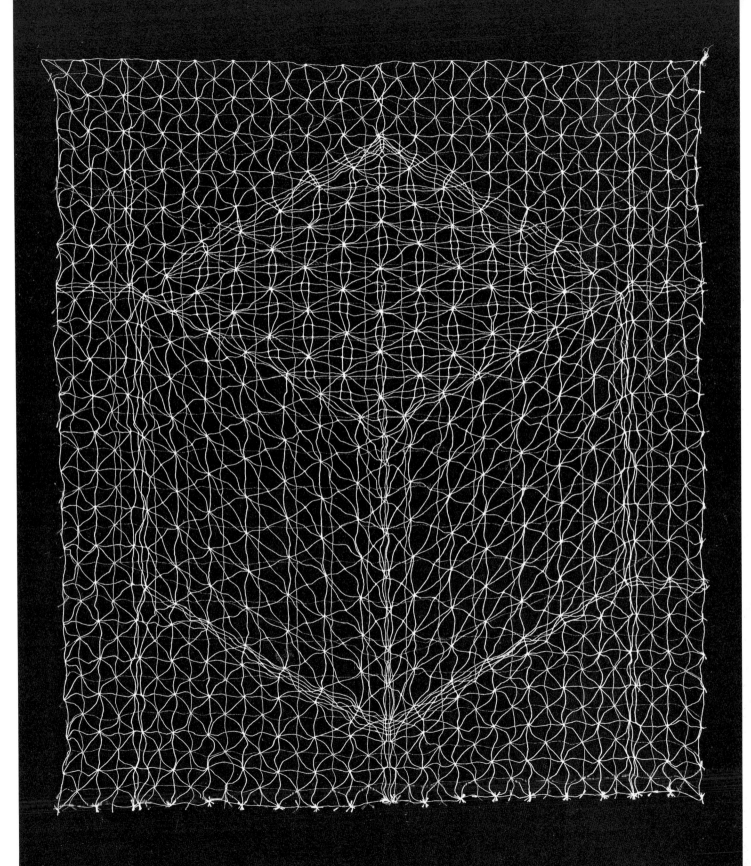

vedge interlacing allows the materials to come across at full force.

To a lesser extent, Rossbach also explored the possibilities offered by the need to darn in the wefts on four-selvedge textiles. Sheila Hicks wove a number of very small such pieces in the early 1960s, also in-spired by Peruvian textiles. They have the wefts interlacing in an irregular way, which is more likely to happen when one is darning than when weaving. These pieces influenced Rossbach, giving him the idea that the interlacing order could change from one part of the piece to another.[58] Among the four-selvedge textiles Rossbach made in the 1970s using cotton welting cord is a small example (1976) made of cord in two different sizes that illustrates this approach.[59] A related piece, **Napkin** (1976), uses elements of one size in plain weave, but with occasional floats.[60] It is folded approximately in quarters as a napkin might be laid on the table after dinner. The four selvedges echo the squareness of the napkin form. Many of Rossbach's other four-selvedge pieces made of welting cord are damasks, so are discussed in this context below.

49. **Equivocal Cube,** 1969
    Plastic
    Bobbin lace
    48″ x 43″
    Collection of the Artist

50. **Bobbin Lace with Openings,** 1970
    Plastic tubing
    Bobbin lace
    20 1/2″ x 44 1/2″
    Collection of the Artist

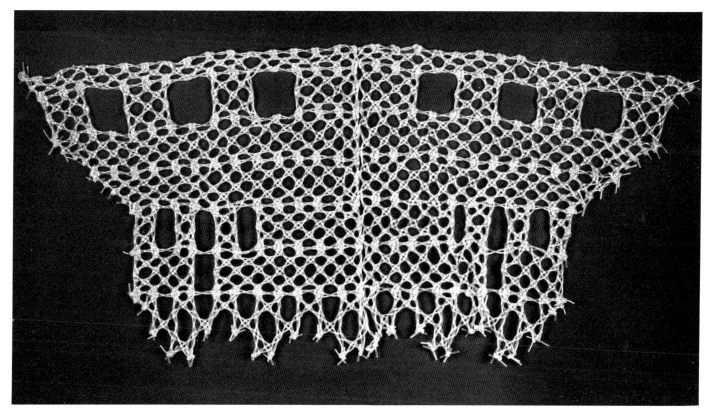

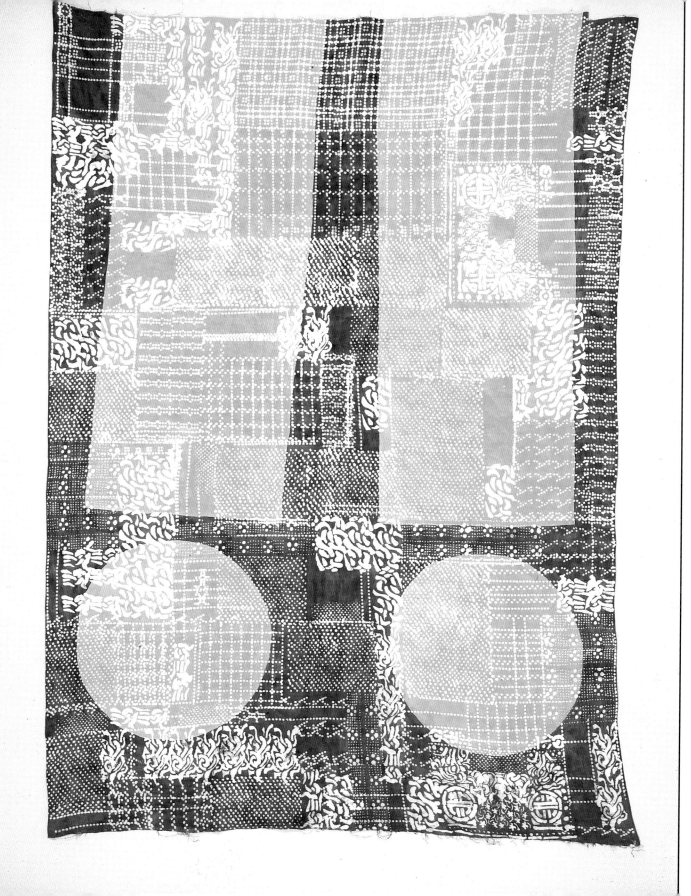

NON-LOOM TECHNIQUES

Rossbach's work from the 1960s displays a tremendous technical diversity. During this period, fiber artists began to revive and explore a variety of non-loom techniques, looking to less mechanized cultures for inspiration. For Rossbach, this was again a natural outgrowth of his teaching and study. Besides the four-selvedge pieces described above, he created works in macrame, braiding, looping, knotted netting, twining, coiling, and plaiting. In the late 1960s and early 1970s he also explored the techniques of needle and bobbin laces.

It is interesting to compare Rossbach's macrame (knotting with a set of elements) with other work of the period. The fad in macrame in the country as a whole was fueled by the publication of Virginia Harvey's book, *Macrame: The Art of Creative Knotting* (N.Y.: Reinhold Pub. Corp.) in 1967. However, Rossbach learned the technique from a Boy Scout manual that Imogene Gieling (a jewelry maker who taught at Berkeley in 1954-61) gave him and he was making pieces as early as 1965. **Ceremonial Plate with Face** (Fig. 28) is one example.

His pieces do not have the top and bottom edges created by the traditional techniques Harvey advocates, with the cords mounted on a single starting horizontal

previous pages, from left:

51. **Homage to Japan,** 1970
    Linen, cotton
    Plain weave, warp and weft ikat
    90″ x 86 1/2″
    Collection of the Artist

52. **Ground Cloth,** 1972
    Commercial cotton fabric, dye
    Stencil resist dyed
    95 1/2″ x 69″
    Collection of the Artist

and finishing in fringe at the bottom. Instead, they are finished in the same way all around, which gives them an entirely different look. In **World Egg**, 1969 (Fig. 43), the starting edge is actually the bottom of the piece and the ends of the cords have been invisibly terminated, while in **Macrame**, 1967 (Fig. 37), no starting edge is apparent at all and the outer edge is fringed all around.[61] Of course these works also eschew the monotonously symmetrical arrangements of knots found in most other pieces of the period.

He also explored three-dimensional forms, as in **Ceremonial Plate with Face** and **Christmas Basket**, 1968 (Fig. 54), to a much greater extent than others at the time and his pieces also have a much more complex and subtle use of color.[62] **Ceremonial Plate with Face** has the facial features formed as much by the change of direction in the knotting as by color, but the flame-like effect around the edge is done with color alone. **Christmas Basket** is made of ribbons and decorations leftover from unwrapped Christmas presents.

Tubular Construction, 1969 (Fig. 42), is both knotted and interlaced in a construction unique to Rossbach. The major elements are braided cotton cords in white, yellow and blue, enclosed in plastic tubing. They interlace each other in an irregular way, but are also tied together by small shiny ribbons (in the same colors as the larger threads) on which are also threaded lengths of opaque white tubing. In the use of knotting and plastic "beads," this piece is related to **World Egg**, though in **World Egg** these elements are the principal components, with the beads forming voids in the fabric. In **Tubular Construction** these elements are subordinate to the braids and add to the complexity of the piece.

Unlike macrame, braiding was not a technique that other artists of the period explored to any great extent. However, it shares some similarities with macrame: it employs a single set of elements, and traditional pieces have a starting edge and finishing fringe as well as a bilaterally symmetrical arrangement of the yarns. Rossbach's approach, related to what he did with macrame in **Macrame**, was to make masses of narrow braids whose elements move between adjacent braids at intervals. The resulting structure is net-like, but the effect is of a more substantial fabric than a net where meshes are formed only by single threads. Greater possibilities also exist for the complex use of color than in a net.

Rossbach made two major pieces in this technique. **New Ireland** (1965) was made after a trip to the Museum fur Volkerkunde in Basel, inspired by the work from New Ireland he had seen there. He recalls immediately beginning to work with all the string and twine he could collect as he traveled.[63] **New Ireland** has a square mesh, with the braids massed to form a denser cross shape within the whole. In the triangular mesh of **Constructed Color**, 1965 (Fig. 34), the denser areas radiate from the center in a more nebulous way.[64] The shape of the mesh is thus appropriate for the design. The coloristic and textural subtleties of these pieces are extraordinary.

This braiding technique also occurs in the upper right corner of his weft-twined **Construction** (1965).[65] Here the braids parallel the warps and wefts, but they also overlie each other in several layers, irregularly connected. On the left the braids turn and become warps for the weft twining. The twining is spaced, so the warp stripes are plainly visible, an effect similar to that found in some Siberian baskets illustrated in *Baskets as Textile Art*.[66] However, he avoids a grid-like effect by taking advantage of the fact

that the warps do not have to be under tension so that some of the wefts can be discontinuous and converge in various places. **Construction** is Rossbach's only major wall piece in weft twining, though the technique is also found in some of his baskets.

Rossbach used archaeological textiles, both Peruvian and Coptic, as design sources as well as technique sources during this period. He feels that the aesthetic enjoyment of a piece is increased by the historical association.[67] However, he liked to change the technique in which the designs were made as well as increase the scale. For example, in **Young Hercules**, 1967 (Fig. 39), he used a Peruvian technique (looping) for a Coptic design which he greatly enlarged.[68] The design of rabbits and grapes is derived from a photograph, taken with a microscope, of a Coptic tapestry in the

53. **Coptic Head,** 1971
    Cotton string, newspaper, paint
    Needlepoint lace
    9″ x 8″
    Collection of the Artist

54. **Christmas Basket,** 1968
Synthetic ribbon, plastic found objects
Macrame
8″ x 6″ x 5″
Mr. and Mrs. Sanford M. Besser, Little Rock, Arkansas

Photo: Vince Foster

56. **Copper Basket,** 1973
Barrier cloth
Diagonal plaiting with shaped elements
9″ x 11″ x 11 1/2″
Collection of the Artist

55. **Tribe of Baskets,** 1970
Polyethylene film tubing
Diagonal plaiting
Size varies with installation (individual baskets: 8″ x
6″ x 6 1/2″; 8″ x 6″ x 6″; 7″ x 6″ x 7″; 6″ x 6″
x 5 1/2″ , 5″ x 3 1/2″ x 3 1/2″)
Collection of the Artist

de Young Museum in San Francisco. He wanted to find out what created the animation in Coptic textile designs. Although looping does not allow the fine detail possible in tapestry weave, the figures do come across with considerable vitality. In addition, he created holes filled in with fine thread to suggest the mounting and repair of archaeological textiles.

Another piece with a Coptic design is **Coptic Veil** (ca. 1968), a knotted net with square mesh that has a design created by knotting in additional colored threads. The effect is similar to the Peruvian embroidery technique used to pattern woven square mesh in Chancay textiles.[69] However, ancient nets rarely have patterns created with color changes. Rossbach's net thus has a design stronger than an archaeological net but more transparent than a tapestry.

The technique in **Early Cross**, 1967 (Fig. 40), is that used in pre-Spanish Peru to make pile caps: square knotting with lengths of yarn inserted in each knot to create the pile.[70] The scale of the technique is much larger in Rossbach's piece than in the Peruvian prototype, but it works well. The effect is similar to but denser than the Coptic weft loop pile technique which is also used for large scale designs. The direction of the knotting changes in several areas to parallel the turning of the corner in the design of the lower and left sides of the piece. He said the design started out as a Coptic head, and then he decided that it looked like the woman (Mrs. Cross) across the street who came out in the morning in a pink bathrobe to get her newspaper. It amuses him for people to think that the title has some esoteric religious meaning. Again, this technique has not been in general use among contemporary fiber artists.

Rossbach also used looping for more abstract effects. **Layered Mesh**, 1970 (Fig. 41), is made with

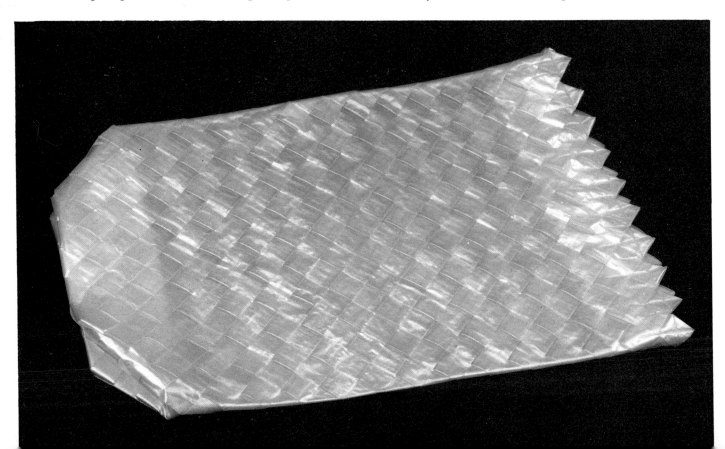

simple looping, done loosely enough so that the result is an open mesh. The looping is in several layers, with the under layers showing through the gaps in the top one. The idea of doing the mesh in multiple layers is original to Rossbach. Traditionally, looping is most often used to make such things as bags and hats. Here several colors of plastic garbage bags are used as the elements, clear, white, brown, blue, and green, and the layering combines these colors in various ways.

Netted Newspaper, 1975 (Fig. 63), is a slightly later piece that approaches the technique of looping in yet a different way.[71] The elements are flattened strips of newspaper encased in polyethylene. The looping structure involves twisting the element, but in this piece all the twists are flattened in a particular way to form regular polygonal shapes, and the voids are polygonal too. The idea of folding newspaper, for instance to make a hat, is appealing to him. The actual structure of this piece is loop and twist with an additional element wrapped spirally around each row.

Newspaper Knot, 1975 (Fig. 61), is the type of minimalist textile statement that Rossbach so enjoys.[72] Here he has crumpled the paper, holding it in place with the string, which allows it to curve.

Needle and bobbin laces are both exacting techniques traditionally made with very fine thread. Rossbach was interested not in recreating the idea of lace but in exploring what the techniques themselves could express on a large scale. Needle lace is based on looping. Threads outlining a design are couched down on paper and looping is used to fill in these designs. We see this concept easily in Coptic Head, 1971 (Fig.

57. **Plastic Bag**, 1970
    Polyethylene film tubing
    Diagonal plaiting
    21″ x 14″
    Collection of the Artist

53), where the drawing and threads form the design with great economy of means. The drawing (on a scrap of the Sunday comics) was originally intended to be a preliminary sketch, but Rossbach said, "I liked the relationship of the lace to the drawing I had made and was supposedly following—it seemed complete so I stopped."[73]

While most traditional laces are monochromatic, **Mickey Mouse Lace**, 1971 (Fig. 72), has the design worked in the appropriate colors. Here too the thread is finer in relation to the density of the looping than in most lace so that the individual loops may be easily read. The sketchiness seems fitting for the character.

Mickey Mouse is a design that occurs in numerous other Rossbach pieces, and examples in coiled basketry, damask, and brocaded silk are also illustrated here. The artist especially likes to use it in techniques that are particularly laborious (such as needle lace and fine coiled basketry) or complex (the damask and brocaded silk), an ironic comment since Mickey Mouse is commonly used by students as a metaphor for something particularly easy or (however unjustified) for textile courses specifically. In addition of course, Rossbach thinks about Mickey Mouse as a contemporary icon and enjoys the identification with popular culture.

Bobbin lace is made with a set of elements in which the threads interlace or interwork in a combination of oblique interlacing and oblique twining. Rossbach made a number of small pieces in this technique using a white vinyl tape, creating asymmetrical abstract designs.[74] The lace shown here, **Bobbin Lace with Openings**, 1970 (Fig. 50), is made of a relatively stiff clear plastic tubing and has a simple symmetrical design. The material gives the piece considerable body, needed in such a large scale piece. The mesh is one of the most basic in bobbin lace, generally called torchon, which creates a diamond grid. However, instead of making diamond shaped designs which would

83

be natural to this ground, Rossbach has contrived a series of square and rectangular lines and voids.

Equivocal Cube, 1969 (Fig. 49), is also bobbin lace, made with white and orange plastic thread. The white thread forms the main design while the orange forms a secondary grid. The technique involves twisting together pairs of threads which interlace at intervals with intersecting pairs. Normally in bobbin lace the crossings are made between two pairs, which intersect either diagonally or horizontally and vertically. When they meet, the bobbin lace technique normally separates the pairs to interlace them and this occurs where two pairs of white meet. But where a white and orange pair intersect, one pair encloses the other in its twist.[75] The interlacing creates a slight bulge at the join, but where the twist is maintained, there is no bulge. Crossings of three pairs occur occasionally in bobbin lace, but Rossbach has managed intersections of four pairs to make the main grid and six pairs on top of the cube. By thus stretching the capacity of the technique he creates both square and diamond grids. The grid changes shape to create the design, itself a square idea visualized in diamond form.

Rossbach also exploited the low melting point property of plastic in making several works that are composed of flat pieces of plastic joined by heat sealing the edges. **Vinyl Log Cabin**, 1970 (Fig. 45), is constructed in strips in the manner of a log cabin quilt.[76] In contrast to **Log Cabin Sham**, the heat sealing technique involves piecing, and thus lends itself very well to pieced quilt designs. However, he deliberately offsets the design in the middle of the piece,

58. **Montaña Poncho,** 1975
    Canvas, newspaper, paint
    Constructed
    48″ x 37″
    Dr. Steven J. Kaplan
    Photo: Richard Eells

which confuses the eye. In comparison, surface interest in a more traditional piece would instead be created by using varied printed fabrics.

Slip Cover for a Computer, 1969 (Fig. 47), was also created by heat sealing plastic. It has much piecing of strips within the transparent areas forming bands of different density. Solid blue and black patches create shapes vaguely reminiscent of sixties-style computer coding. Although most of the seals are on the back, some are on the front, and the flaps add to the texture. Red ribbons (openers from cellophane wrappings) and black cords are trapped within pockets of plastic. Snippets of commercial food wrappers with red and yellow printing are interspersed; the only legible image is the round blue and yellow Sungod logo in the upper right area. These round images are balanced by the pieced rayed section in the lower left.

PLAITING

Rossbach explored plaiting techniques extensively during the 1970s.[77] In a 1973 article he notes that this technique is fast, large scale and conducive to many seamless three-dimensional shapes and surface treatments.[78] Most of his 1970s plaited pieces were made of paper or plastic. He made both flat wall pieces and baskets. The wall pieces interpret this technique in a wide variety of ways.[79]

His pieces with horizontal and vertical elements relate to the four-selvedge textiles discussed earlier. Several are made of plastic tubing and the edges are simply finished with heat sealing. In **Jet X 10**, 1971 (Fig. 48), the tubing is filled with such things as plastic yarns, pieces of styrofoam trays, styrofoam packing chips, plastic straws cut up, and pieces of a child's toy airplane picked up on the street, which is the source of the title. These items create a lively texture while the blue grid unifies the piece.

In **Reconstituted Commercial Textile**, 1960 (Fig.

85

59. **Raffia Basket and Pitcher,** 1973
Raffia, local palm
Twined
10″ x 7″ x 7″ (basket)
10″ x 10″ x 6″ (pitcher)
Milwaukee Art Museum, Purchase
Photo: Richard Eells

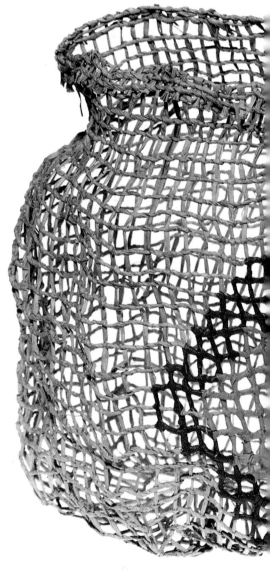

23), he first tied and discharged (bleached) a brown and white striped fabric. This fabric was then torn into strips, some parallel to the stripes and some perpendicular. The strips were inserted in plastic tubing, and then interlaced in a manner approximating their original position in the fabric. But the composition becomes more interesting as the stripes are broken up by each of these processes (discharge, tearing and interlacing). In half of the piece the stripes interlace since both vertical and horizontal elements are torn parallel to the stripes; while in the other half, the stripes all appear parallel since half are torn perpendicular to the stripes. The effect is again optically challenging.

Plaited Handgun, 1975 (Fig. 75), has a startling representational image. Rossbach says of this design:

> When I put an image of a handgun in my work . . . I was almost certainly influenced by a painting I had seen reproduced in an art magazine. It didn't strike me at the time as a neat idea for a piece of plaiting. In fact I have forgotten that experience entirely but I'm sure it took place. Later, in looking through the newspaper I saw a photo of the gun used in the Kennedy assassination. It spoke to me. I xeroxed it after it had been lying around my table for a while, and enlarged it. Then I drafted it on graph paper, and also on a diagonal graph. I like the graphs as much as I like the plaiting. Then I plaited a handgun image.[80]

The image is created in oblique interlacing using the damask principle (in 4/1 satin), but the effect is much like the dots in a printed photograph.[81] It is thus a perfect blend of design and technique, although one does not expect to see such a brutal image conveyed in a playful medium like plaited paper.

Plaited Handgun is one of several plaited pieces Rossbach made in two layers with the elements folding around the sides and through slits in the middle of the piece. Another example is **Window** (1975), which is actually padded on the inside, most prominently next to the slits, drawing the eye to this area.[82] The piece is made of strips of cloth and paper, the loose ends of which give the piece further dimensionality. He interlaces striped paper on one diagonal with solid color strips in the other. The stripes are perpendicular to the elements, and in some light is predominant and in others dark. Occasional floats further break up the regularity of the surface.

Drop Cloth, 1975 (Fig. 62), is also two-layer with cotton wadding inside it here and there in a rhythm with the holes. The holes come naturally to the mat-making technique but are not commonly found in ethnographic mats because of their impracticality in use. The square orientation of the holes correlates with the outlines of the piece but their arrangement in a slightly off of vertical lineup relates them to the diagonal path of the elements. The piece is made of strips from a painter's drop cloth, a somewhat odd but actually beautiful and strong material.

In **Peruvian Tunic**, 1976 (Fig. 69), Rossbach worked from a black and white photograph of a very elaborate late Nasca textile in The Metropolitan Museum of Art (Fig. 68), replicating its effect in canvas and newspaper but not its extremely complex technique.[83] Actually, the Peruvian textile as photographed is pieced in a way that does not reflect its original form. The crosswise seams that are visible in the plain areas would not be there if the piece were in original condition. Some ambiguity also exists about the attachment of the fringe, especially to the plain areas. The neck slot is cut rather than woven in, so the piece was not even originally a tunic and is in any case longer in its proportions than genuine Peruvian tunics are.

Rossbach's piece does not reproduce these discrepancies and is therefore a more unified composition. His lengthening of the interlaced bands and adding fringe to the plain sections contrasts with the Peruvian piece but is visually more logical. The piece

is also not as monochromatic as it appears in a black and white photograph: colored newspaper and blue string were used for the braided bands. The canvas strips between the braided bands are slightly rumpled, with brown stains on top of the crinkles, as would be found in an archaeological textile. He block printed and tie dyed the cloth in the fringe in yellow, red, and black.

BASKETS

Perhaps his most influential work has been in basketry, not only through the many baskets he has made and his teaching but also through his two books on the subject, *Baskets as Textile Art* (1973, reprinted in 1986 as *The Nature of Basketry*), an appreciation of historical baskets, and *The New Basketry* (1976), which surveys the development of contemporary fiber art as it leads to baskets. His preoccupation with this

subject is not surprising, given a background in ceramics (vessel forms), the links between the department in which he was teaching at Berkeley and the fabulous basket collection at the Lowie Museum of Anthropology, his preference for making personal-sized art, and his interest in exploring many different textile techniques and materials.

Rossbach speaks in the introduction to *Baskets as Textile Art* of his desire to make a basket from the grasses of the Aleutian Islands while he was stationed there in the army, but the earliest piece he did that could be described as a basket was not consciously done as a basket. It was instead an exploration of what came naturally to materials he was interested in using, a palm leaf whose fronds he used as warp for weft-faced interlacing in ixtle and plastic raffia (1957).[84] His first baskets in 1964 were also the result of experimenting with various techniques and materials, rather than following a basketry handbook.

60. **Coiled Newspaper Basket,**
 1974
 Newspaper, polyethylene film
  tubing, cotton string
 Coiled
 6″ x 8″ x 8″
 Collection of the Artist

61. **Newspaper Knot,** 1975
 Newspaper, polyethylene film
  tubing, plastic string
 Knotted
 6″ x 10 1/2″ x 1″
 Collection of the Artist
 Photo: Emil Ghinger

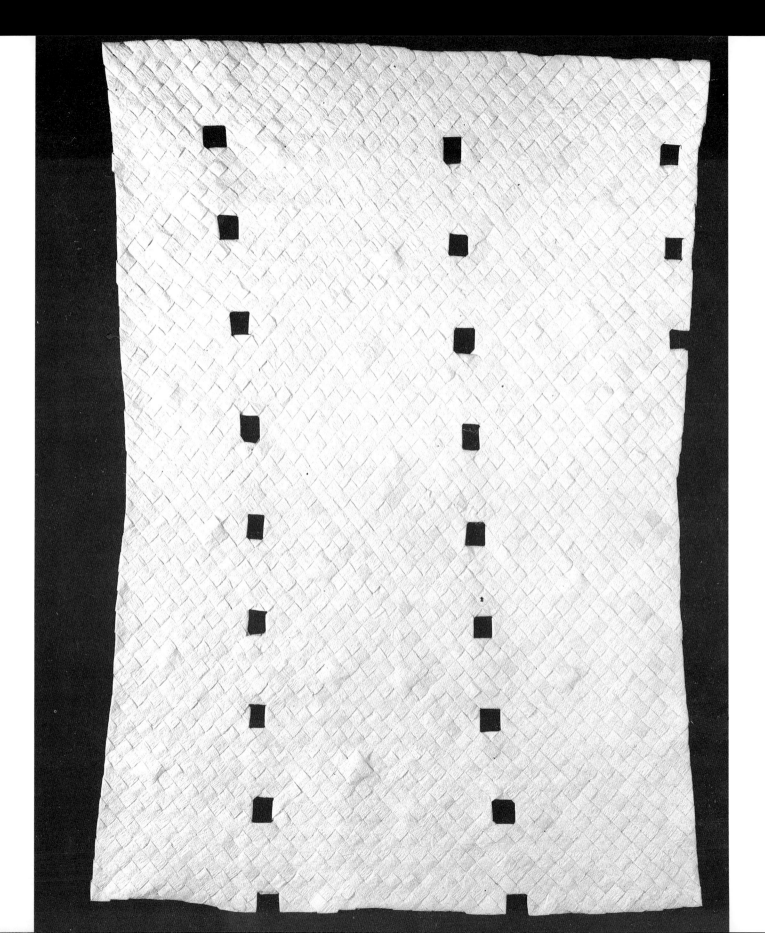

62. **Drop Cloth,** 1975
    Commercially manufactured
        painter's drop cloth (plastic
        coated paper), cotton
    Diagonal plaiting in two lay-
        ers, stuffed
    63 1/2″ x 46 1/2″
    Collection of the Artist

63. **Netted Newspaper,** 1975
    Newspaper, polyethylene film
        tubing
    Looping, wrapping
    36″ x 31″
    Collection of the Artist

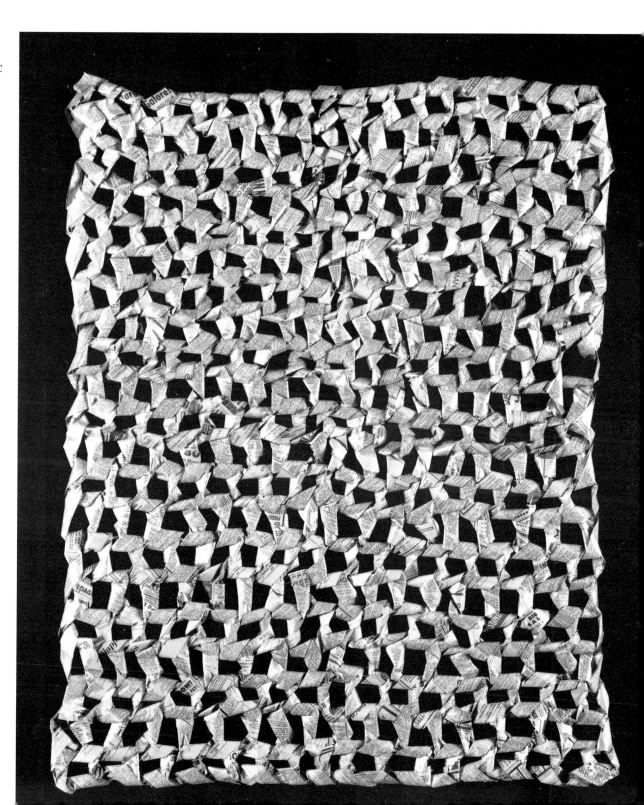

Two of these early baskets, **Hornets' Nest** and **Looped Cylinder** (Fig. 26-27), are shown here. **Hornets' Nest** is coiled, a common basketry technique, but made in an odd shape. Rossbach says, "When it was constructed, it looked too new, so I rubbed gesso into the outer surface, making it rather dusty looking. I also embroidered the surface in a few places—sort of implying the mending on old baskets."[85] He does in fact respond aesthetically to wear in old textiles.[86] About **Looped Cylinder**, he says, "I didn't expect it to be so cockeyed. I had dyed the rattan, which took the color poorly. The effect was quite drab. From being manipulated in the netting technique, the rattan became rough and fibrous." It certainly is an unconventional piece.

Basket with Handle, 1966 (Fig. 29), was inspired by the baskets from Ischia in Italy that have wire frames wrapped with raffia and different kinds of interlacing filling in the gaps.[87] Rossbach used a lampshade frame turned upside down as a foundation for this piece, but his patches of interlacing divide off of each other in a much more complex and fantastical way than the basic frame suggests. Some of the other non-loom techniques he was exploring in the 1960s also lent themselves to three-dimensional forms, including macrame (**Christmas Basket**) and looping (**Netted Bottles**).[88]

Rossbach then set out to learn basketry techniques according to orthodox procedures:

> After I had made a number of baskets of improvised techniques, I settled down and followed directions in a book on basketmaking. I learned to do twining, wickerwork, etc., and became able to make neat rims. I did a series of these traditional baskets out of rattan. I exhibited them only once, in Bellingham, Washington, in 1967 . . . I discovered that the more skillful I became, the more standard the baskets appeared.[89]

Knit Reeds, 1967 (Fig. 30), though also of rattan, is hardly standard. Rossbach had found a diagram of the machine knit structure usually called tricot in *American Fabrics* magazine.[90] He made a template and bent the wet rattan around a series of nails, letting it dry in this shape. Afterwards he assembled the elements, though the structure was so stretchy that it had to be tied together in places around the rim.

In *Baskets as Textile Art* he explains the principles of the construction of the melon basket, which is unusual among baskets in having a rigid skeleton constructed first, later filled in with interlacing.[91] He seems to have been fascinated by this idea and around 1968 made a number of baskets in which the skeleton is totally exposed.[92] Instead of solid opaque interlacing he wraps transparent plastic or rawhide around the basket's ribs.

In the coiled cornhusk basket he made in 1969, the cornhusk and split reed coils are large and the cotton string binding sparse so that the cornhusks are indeed the major essence of the piece.[93] Although the horizontal coils are visible at the top and bottom of the basket, Rossbach has sewed vertical bunches of cornhusk over the convex sides. This is a novel way to decorate a coiled basket, though technically congruent with the rest of the piece. Besides adding visual interest to the piece the extra stitching probably also helps support it.

In the 1970s he further explored techniques traditionally associated with basketry, particularly plaiting (interlacing), but also coiling and twining. In addition to the advantages of plaiting noted above, it seems that its appeal also lay with the fact that the material is an important component of the object's final finished effect since the elements used are relatively unmodified.[94] Inspired by the anthropological literature, Rossbach explored a variety of plant materials for plaiting, including iris, palm, cattails, tules, and most notably New Zealand flax. His wife Katherine has

64. Large Twined Basket with Four Handles, 1976
Newspaper, masking tape
Twined, interlaced
7″ x 19″ x 20 1/2″
Collection of the Artist

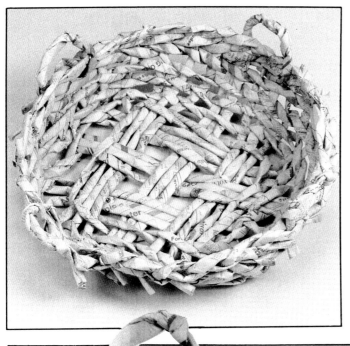

detailed his fruitless search for the palms so often used for plaiting in tropical climates.[95] New Zealand flax grew in his backyard so he was able to use this more extensively, although the slivers he acquired in his fingertips from splitting the leaves eventually required surgery.[96] He enjoyed using the leaves green, and then watching the basket dry out rather than drying the materials first.

Of course he also used contemporary materials, such as newspapers, cotton cloth, flattened plastic tubing, blue-print linen, corrugated paper, anodized aluminum, mylar, ribbon, flagging tape, etc. The components of **Tribe of Baskets,** 1970 (Fig. 55), are made with flattened plastic tubing, as is **Plastic Bag,** 1970 (Fig. 57).[97] The interlacing in these baskets is perfectly plain: we see here again his delight in ''simple, clearly stated, structural relationships.''[98] The baskets complement each other in their different proportions, different sizes of elements. The plastic material is shiny, luminous.

His 1972 **Irrelevant Solution** and **Soft Construction** were made in plain diagonal interlacing of folded

strips of newspaper.[99] Actually sculptures of packages rather than baskets due to their lack of openings, they have string around them as packages do, though the string here helps the empty forms keep their shape. Their emptiness creates their soft contours and weightlessness. Although the interlacing is simple, the print on the newspaper creates a lively texture. The print runs in the same direction as the elements, so that it intersects as well as the strips. The size of these pieces was to a great extent conditioned by the size of newspaper.

Copper Basket, 1973 (Fig. 56), made of barrier cloth, another shiny material, was inspired by an Iroquois basket belonging to Lea Miller in which the elements are larger at the bottom of the basket.[100] However, in the prototype, the change is somewhat abrupt, creating an angle between the base and the neck, whereas in Rossbach's piece the change is gradual, creating a gently swelling form.

In **Rag Basket**, 1973 (Fig. 66), made of cloth wrapped around strips of corrugated cardboard for stiffening, he plays with the possibilities of color mixing offered by this technique, with the elements changing color partway along their length.[101] The raw edges of the fabric, which he does not systematically hide, add to the textural effect. The curved intersecting bands seem to come out of the plaiting, but contrast with it not only because of the curves but also by the fact that they do not interlace each other, as signalled by the dotted pop art style shadows.

In **Cairn**, 1973 (Fig. 65), he took advantage of the sculptural possibilities of plaiting and constructed a form that looks like a pile of irregularly shaped granite boulders used to mark wilderness trails. He uses elements of white cloth strips, speckled (by silk screening) in black, and stiffened by a backing of paper (the type with a sticky back that can be ironed on). These strips are interlaced in over-one under-one order and turn at right angles three-dimensionally at

places other than edges to make the bumps in the form, a technique also used to create the shape of **Butterfly Basket**, 1973 (Fig. 67). Although the technique is traditionally used to shape the bottom of baskets, it is seldom exploited to make a more elaborately sculptural form.[102] The rabbit is from a woodblock the Rossbachs bought in Iran which he used in other textiles as well.[103]

Although the red butterfly design on **Butterfly Basket** looks from a distance as if it were put on after the basket was plaited, closer examination reveals that in fact the elements were colored first. The designs used on the cloth were squares and dots, thus relating to the modules formed by the plaiting. These designs are apparent in the final product, but the cutting into strips and subsequent interlacing scrambles them in interesting ways.

Raffia Basket and Pitcher, 1973 (Fig. 59), are made with weft twining, but with extra twists between the warps which hold them apart and make a sort of grid.[104] The basket has a design made by wrapping a supplementary dark element around the twined grid. The loose construction allows the nature of the materials to assert themselves. It amuses Rossbach that this pitcher is utterly incapable of holding water.

Rossbach also made twined baskets out of newspaper, as in **Large Twined Basket with Four Handles**, 1976 (Fig. 64).[105] Putting four handles on a basket seems logical enough in terms of its form, but one also realizes that since humans have only two hands, the extra handles are not functional even conceptually. Of course this basket is too fragile for use anyway.

He also made coiled baskets with newspaper, as in **Coiled Newspaper Basket**, 1974 (Fig. 60), but in these pieces the newspaper is wrapped in plastic.[106] The material is substantial enough so that a sparse binding of colored string is sufficient, giving prominence to the newspaper. Ribs up the sides also provide stability. **Minnie Mouse**, 1975 (Fig. 70), has a design added in vinyl tape. The imbrication of vinyl tape on the surface of the coils, caught down under the bindings, changes the look of the piece entirely, emphasizing the module of the bindings instead of the foundation coils.

Mickey Mouse Coil Basket, 1975 (Fig. 73), on the other hand, is worked on a much finer scale with much finer materials, and again illustrates the use of this design with a laborious technique.[107] Mickey Mouse's pose and the parallelogram rather than square frame in which he stands oppose the direction of the spiral structure of the basket but at the same time balance it.

A Japanese influence is evident in his baskets by the 1980s; many are plaited (interlaced) of ash splints which may be covered on the outside in rice paper and/or lacquer. These treatments add richness to the surface without totally obscuring the underlying structure. These papered and lacquered baskets may have been inspired by such Japanese baskets as the one covered with gold foil illustrated in *Baskets as Textile Art*.[108] Although Rossbach's baskets do not have large holes that need filling in as does the foil-covered Japanese basket, he obviously responded to the sheen of the paper and the way it emphasized the structure.

Rossbach's plaited baskets often have interesting structural effects. The cylindrical baskets may have the elements splitting part way up the side or have changes in the order of interlacing or both, as in **Progression** and **Fancy Plaid**, both 1983 (Figs. 95 & 91).[109] In **Fancy Plaid**, the diagonal color bands, correlating with the size of the base, might give the piece a giddy swirling effect, but the composition is stabilized by the newspaper applique strips and the red lacquer on the rim. **Tangerine**, 1988 (Fig. 96), has extra vertical and horizontal elements on the lower part.[110] The photograph actually shows the narrower side of this rectangular piece.

New World Egg, 1985 (Fig. 87), is a randomly interlaced sphere covered with rice paper that has a heat transfer image of a skull pasted over it. The basket gives the skull its three dimensional quality, the rice paper its whiteness. The egg shape of the piece and the skull image contain in one object the beginning and end of life. The piece is associated in his mind with his much earlier macrame **World Egg**, presumably because of the approximately egg shape.

Rossbach also finds rectangular shapes satisfying to plait with ash splints. **Purple Box**, 1985 (Fig. 79), has two colors of elements alternating both vertically and horizontally, making either vertical (on the narrow sides) or horizontal (on the wider sides) stripes, a principle familiar to any weaver from the log cabin design.[111] **Treasury**, 1982 (Fig. 92), uses a related principle, in which the elements themselves are ribbed (corrugated cardboard), thus creating a "log cabin" effect.

Lettuce Basket, 1982 (Fig. 80), has a chunky irregular form plaited with newspaper and then covered with rice paper and lacquered.[112] The newspaper is obviously more capable of taking this complex shape than ash splints, and its softness is reflected in the form even though the print has been obliterated.

Rossbach has also made a variety of baskets and related sculptures by tying sticks together. **John Travolta**, 1978 (Fig. 78), is made in this way.[113] Rossbach credits its inspiration to the book *How to Wrap Five Eggs*, which presents the various ingenious methods of Japanese packaging.[114] He made the stand in order to raise the sheer textile so that light would pass through the image. The **Origami Basket with Mickey Mouse**, before 1981 (Fig. 81), also reflects an obvious Japanese inspiration.[115] The image of Mickey Mouse, which unfortunately does not show in the photograph, is inside the basket.

Eagle's Nest Box, 1984 (Fig. 90), has a specific source, according to the artist:

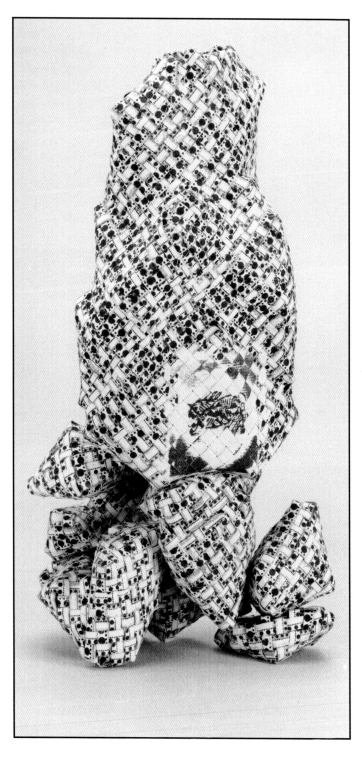

When Katherine and I were in Juneau, Alaska, we saw an eagle's nest in the local museum. As I remember it, it was displayed in a sort of diorama in a stairwell—very close to the stairs—so that as you moved up the stairs you kept seeing the nest from various positions, with a great stuffed eagle hovering over. There was tremendous vigor in the rugged branches and twigs that loosely formed the nest. And of course the eagle was very dramatic, so close at hand.[116]

A nest basket of twigs is included in *Baskets as Textile Art*, so obviously he was also aware of the idea of twig baskets from other sources.[117] The green stand in Rossbach's piece suggests a tree by its elevation and greenness, but also elevates it as a work of art by its pedestal shape.

El Salvador (Fig. 86), a sculpture made for *Fiberarts* magazine in 1984, is representative of his protest baskets, which "try to express my sadness over the killing of young people, and the destruction of their countries."[118] In this case he made something like a shrine to someone who has died. Of the materials that *Fiberarts* sent him he used the camouflage net (draped over the top) and some white cloth which he dyed in broad areas of yellow, green, and red, with a linoleum block printed motif at one end to suggest a flag, and then folded as for a funeral. It pleased him that the pattern of the flag was concealed inside the folds, never to be seen. The wooden stand and plastic flowers he made as a setting for these fabrics.

In about 1986 he started making stapled baskets, using eucalyptus bark, palm bark, Mexican bark paper, wood veneer, or paper and cardboard of various

65. **Cairn,** 1973
Cotton, paper
Silk screened, plaited
24" x 10" x 10"
Collection of the Artist

Rag Basket, 1973
Commercial fabric, corrugated paper
Silk screened, diagonal plaiting
10″ x 12″ x 9 1/2″
Collection of the Artist

Butterfly Basket, 1973
Commercial cotton fabric, paper
Silk screened, diagonal plaiting
10″ x 12″ x 9 1/2″
Dr. and Mrs. Edward Okun
Photo: Mark Katzman

kinds, including commercial food packaging and magazine pages. The material can be cut and folded in various ways to create both regular and irregular volumes. He often adds other surface decoration such as paint, tapes or heat transfer designs. In the baskets of commercial papers, the printing on the cardboard becomes part of the design of the basket (see for example, **Eskimo Pie**, 1987, Fig. 89).[119] Rossbach says that he enjoys seeing what happens when a pattern is transferred from one medium to another. He also admires the commercial lettering and likes not being too serious.[120]

These baskets perhaps come the closest to what Rossbach describes as temporary baskets in *Baskets as Textile Art*. Such baskets are made on the spot from handy natural materials such as large leaves quickly folded and tied to carry home something that has just been hunted or gathered. Once home has been reached, the materials are simply thrown away. These baskets obviously have great appeal to Rossbach, since they retain the natural look of the materials used, and employ spontaneous, simple and direct methods of construction.

Several of the bark baskets shown (**Dark Indian and Buffalo Basket** 1987 and **Bison/Bison** 1988, Figs. 3, 101, 100) have heat transfer designs on them. The brown color and rough texture of the material and the volume of the basket complement these designs in somewhat the same way as the uneven walls of European cave paintings give dimension to the animals painted on them. The faded red fabric lining the inside rim of **Bison/Bison** looks like the sort of 19th century calico that was used in the Old West, as does the gingham on the outside rim of **Dark Indian.**

COMPLEX LOOM TECHNIQUES

At the same time that Rossbach was working so extensively with plaiting in the 1970s, he was also explor-

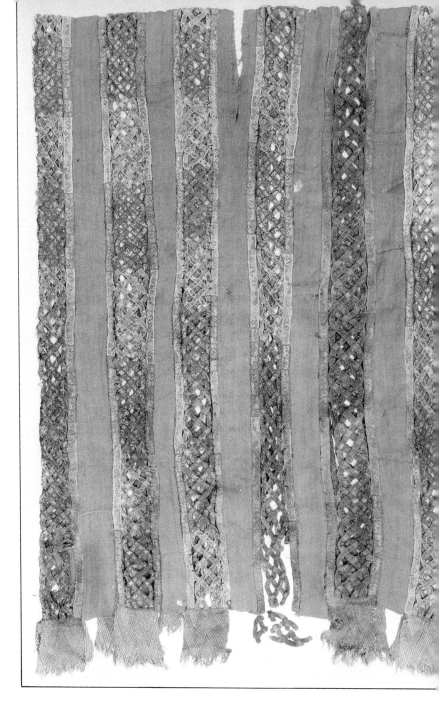

68. **Late Nasca Style Textile, South Coast of Peru,** 500 - 700 A.D.
 Camelid fiber
 Bands of plain weave, double woven complementary-
  warp weave
 The Metropolitan Museum of Art
 Gift of George D. Pratt, 1930
 Photo: The Metropolitan Museum of Art

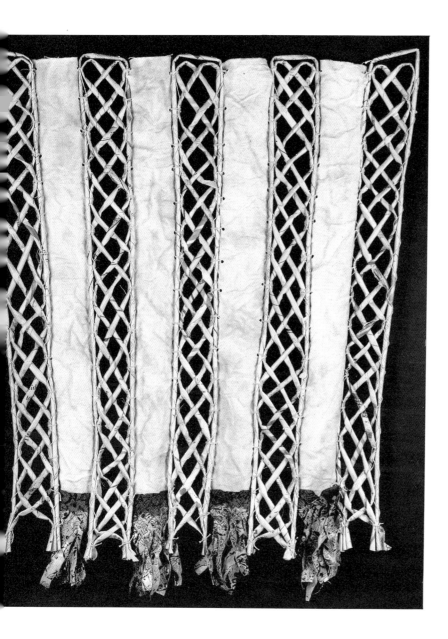

69. **Peruvian Tunic,** 1976
   Commercial cotton fabric, newspaper, cotton string,
      masking tape, dye
   Rolled, plaited, sewn, block printed
   42″ x 56″
   Collection of the Artist

ing techniques designed for weaving fine silk threads on complex looms. He did considerable historical research on European Paisley shawls, woven in the 19th century on drawlooms and then on Jacquard looms, and on 18th century French silks woven on drawlooms. He even had the University buy a drawloom and tried weaving on it, because he wanted to understand how it worked. However, he found it extremely difficult.[121]

To weave the silks shown in Fig. 77 (1976), he used a 16 harness table loom, sometimes taking advantage of all the harnesses and sometimes not. The structure used has a twill ground and supplementary wefts in three-span floats in diagonal (i.e. twill) alignment. This structure keeps the fine supplementary wefts on the surface of the fabric as much as possible, particularly important since the designs in some cases were created by a heat transfer image on the weft.[122] He spread the wefts on a piece of cardboard, holding the turns at the edge with pins, transferred the design and then wove the piece. A fine element is needed to make the images from the heat transfer show. The effect of the heat transfer reminds him of old paintings with crackle in them. One is reminded of his aesthetic appreciation of wear on old textiles and his efforts to obtain diffuse patterning in ikats. In other examples he used ikat, block printing, stencilling or painting to pattern the weft before weaving, as in **Cranes Fly** (Fig. 77e), in which the weft was painted. Apparently the rather strange subject was a reaction to the crane imagery his students were using at one time.[123]

Some of his small table-loom silks have discontinuous wefts, either covering the whole surface or leaving some areas of the ground showing in order to clarify the image. Most of the examples shown in Fig. 77 fall into this category. **Katherine and Tyrone** (Tyrone is the dog) and **Mad Ludwig** have the pattern woven with colored supplementary wefts and then a dark heat transfer design over the finished fabric. The

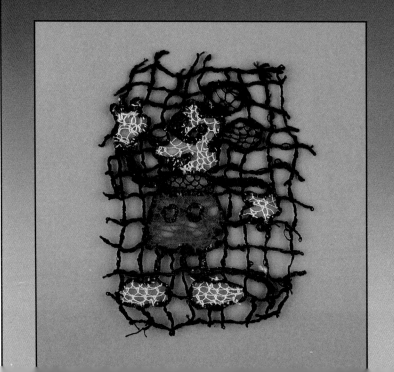

100

weaving provides texture and color while the heat transfer provides detailing to the overall effect. **Katherine and Tyrone** and **18th Century Floral** have light colored linear design elements formed by floating the ground weft for short spaces. **Homage to Boris Kroll** uses red or blue ground wefts instead of the cream colored ones found in the other examples. Kroll is a prominent textile designer.

Others of the small silks in Fig. 77 have all their design in the weaving and exploit the full capabilities of the loom's 16 harnesses and varied treadling possibilities. **Mickey Mouse** and **Spot II** have an elaborate diamond twill background weave, and the designs

have supplementary wefts in longer floats secured with zigzag or diamond patterns. Thus again Mickey Mouse is woven in as elaborate a technique as possible.

Rossbach also explored the damask technique, in which a satin weave is turned so that the warp-float face of the weave creates the background while the weft-float face creates the pattern (or vice versa). Rossbach says of this structure: ''Mostly I am intrigued by the absolute purity of the damask structure for creating imagery—with a balance of identical warp and weft nothing concealed—everything structural, and all the energy of the warps and wefts expressed as they appear as required on the surface.''[124] **Damask Mickey Mouse**, 1976 (Fig. 71), was woven on a table loom with pickup to create the design and is thus another complex weaving of this personification of the simple.[125] He has used a white warp and yellow weft to make the design show clearly.

Rossbach also made a number of large scale damasks with cotton welting cord, many with four selvedges.[126] Some examples have no color or a wash of

previous pages, from left:

70. **Minnie Mouse,** 1975
Newspaper, vinyl tape, cotton string
Coiled with imbrication
16″ x 6″ x 6″
Collection of A. Sarazin, Milwaukee, Wisconsin
Photo: Richard Eells

71. **Damask Mickey Mouse,** 1976
Linen
5/1 Damask
14″ x 13 1/2″
Collection of the Artist

72. **Mickey Mouse Lace,** 1971
Cotton
Needlepoint lace
3 1/2″ x 3″
Collection of the Artist

73. **Mickey Mouse Coil Basket,** 1975
Synthetic raffia, sea grass
Coiled with imbrication
6″ x 9″ x 9″
Jim Harris
Photo: Mark Katzman

74. Book
The Weaver's Secret Book, 1977
Ink on Paper
Drawn, folded, typed, heat transfer printed, collaged
5″ x 5 1/2″ x 3/4″
Collection of the Artist

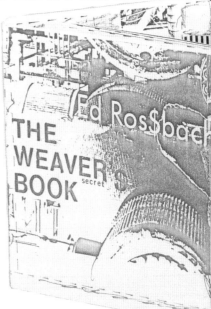

color added after the interlacing was completed. The objective again was to make the structure large enough to register as part of the subject of the work. Rossbach takes another approach in **Damask Waterfall**, 1977 (Fig. 83), and enlivens the surface of the damask check by wrapping the wefts in brightly colored fabric, black tape, and sometimes clear plastic. The piece is another of his favorites.

His work with Jacquard weaving began with a program at the Rhode Island School of Design in Providence in which their power Jacquard loom and technician were made available to fiber artists to produce fabrics for an exhibition held in 1982.[127] This initial experience gave Rossbach other ideas he wanted to try so he has returned to the school several times to do further work. The Jacquard loom is a different kind of challenge for contemporary fiber artists because of the small size of the design repeat (4 1/16″). Rossbach's explorations include changing the structure part way through the weaving, changing patterns (cards) as well as treating the piece after it comes off the loom, for instance adding applique or tie dye. In the example illustrated, **Maine Coast**, 1988 (Fig. 97), he used overspun wefts which contract when dipped in water and produce a puckered effect. The design seems abstract, but was inspired by islands off the coast of Maine. The puckering is thus appropriate for representing the three-dimensionality of the rocks and the ripples of the water.

CONCLUSION

One of Rossbach's favorite quotations is from a book on modern design by Edgar Kaufmann, Jr., head of the Dept. of Industrial Design at the Museum of Modern Art for many years. Kaufmann said, ''Now as always, the greatest delight a fabric can give comes from the structure, the way threads support one another to create a cloth.''[128] Although this statement was written with reference to the utilitarian textiles of the forties, Rossbach ventured to use it also for baskets and it can be applied also to his own work, since it is often the structure that is the key to the meaning of his pieces, which gives us such delight.

ED ROSSBACH: EDUCATOR
Lia Cook

had been teaching for a number of years when I invited Ed Rossbach to come and do something with my class at California College of Arts and Crafts. I didn't know what to expect, although I was eager to be an observer and participant once again rather than the leader. Always being the teacher has its rewards, yet I longed for an earlier time when I could arrive in class with nothing definite about the subject on my mind, just curious, carried away by some new stimulus or spark of an idea. So many students today seem much more businesslike and very serious, intent on building their careers and mostly interested in becoming a "professional." I didn't know, then, exactly what would happen when these students met Ed Rossbach. I hoped some of the magic, some of the intense focus and exhilaration I had often felt as a student in his classroom would infect them too.

Ed greeted me with box in hand as we walked together toward the class. It was a fond and familiar sight as he had rarely entered a class empty-handed, and I found myself anticipating again the day's revelations. When we arrived he began pulling from his box some textiles that looked like old Sears and Roebuck rejects. The chenille weavings were jarring in their awful shades of chartreuse, with sticks and other shiny material stuck in them. They were old and faded. The students looked on in disgust and confusion, but, not wanting to embarrass their honored guest, they tried to keep an open mind. I was perhaps even more disgusted than they, as the colors were the favorite of my mother's generation and my least favorite.

As Rossbach pulled these things out of his box, he talked about his perceptions of the moment and of the past. Feeling them one by one and flinging them out on the table, he exclaimed, "Now what do you think of these? Aren't they wonderful? Aren't they just wonderful?" Of course nobody in the room, least of all me, thought they were wonderful. But soon we were listening intently, swept up in stories and remembrances from the past, mingled with impressions of the moment. As it turned out, the work was none other than that of Dorothy Liebes, one of the most well-known weavers of the 40s, someone whose vibrant personality and experimental works had inspired a generation of Americans.

Rossbach had visited Dorothy Liebes' studio when he had first arrived in the Bay Area. (See Brite/Caldwell discussion.) He told us how he had been fascinated with Dorothy Liebes when he first visited her studio and how he had been in awe of the things she stuck in her warp, of her whole personality, and of how she interacted with those who worked for her. Something happened as he spoke of his personal impressions, connecting vignettes from the past with the immediate presence of the textiles. We began

75. **Plaited Handgun**, 1975
Construction paper
Diagonal plaiting in two layers
36 1/2" x 50"
Collection of the Artist

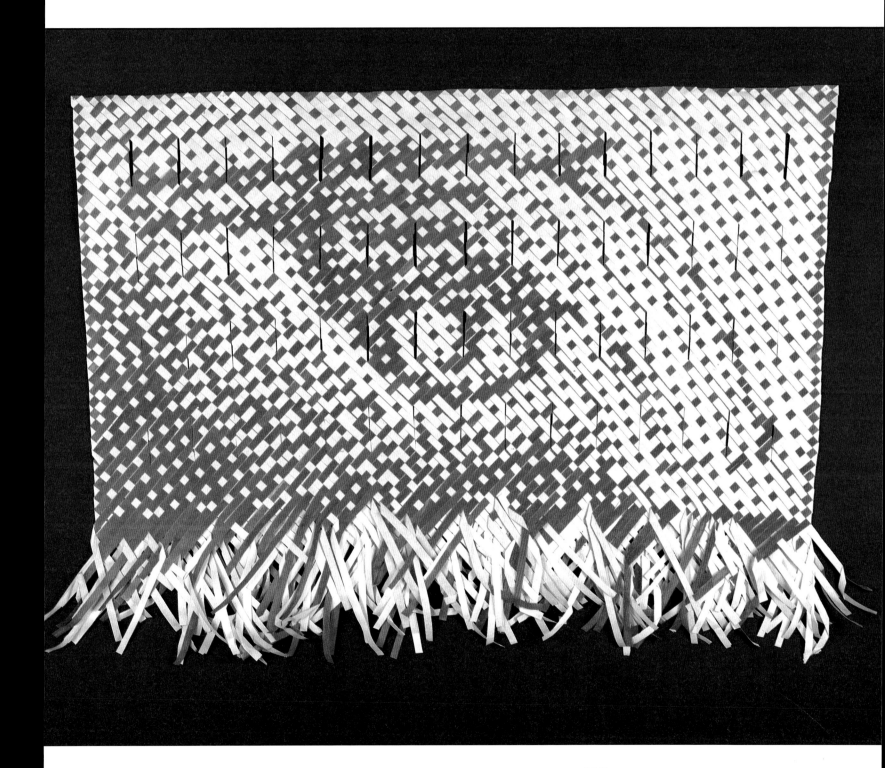

to look beyond our immediate biases to see the textiles as individuals, each possessed of nuance and with histories which could make a valid and vital claim on our interest. We could appreciate that what was commonplace and even ugly to us could once have been exciting and adventurous. We didn't even know whether he liked these things or not; he wanted to know how we responded and what we thought of them. It had been as if time had slowed down a bit. We'd been drawn into his spell, and we all left that classroom, students and teacher alike, looking at the things we had previously taken for granted around us in a new way and in sharper focus.

He hadn't shown any flashy slides nor discussed all his latest ideas. Nor had we discovered any more details about him as an artist than we knew already. What we did get was a glimpse inside another creative mind, one with a fresh way of looking at things. Something personal had been communicated, a curiosity about and a love for textiles, both their past and present.

Years had passed since I had been Ed's student, entranced by these musings and emerging from his classroom invigorated and thoughtful. Myself the teacher now, I find my own musings frequently return to the question, ''What makes a teacher good?'' On the occasion of Ed's visit, I was presented with possible answers, striking in their simplicity and sincerity. As a teacher I know what I believe philosophically; getting these ideas across is another matter again. I may think I am doing one thing, but sometimes the students don't think so or don't appear to get it at all. Rossbach got what he wanted across not by telling us directly, but by doing and being a certain way: open and open-ended, questioning, passionate, honest and vulnerable. He had shared something personal of himself, from the past and of the moment.

Having been a part of the craft revival of the 60s and early 70s in the San Francisco Bay Area, I thought it important that some sort of documentation occur of the time, place and people. Some has been written about the Bay Area ceramic movement, both nationally and internationally, but very little has appeared on the fiber movement. I was caught up and participated in the great surge of energy, creativity, experimentation, and openness that expanded the definition of the textile arts. Contributing much to this expansive and energizing atmosphere was the Design Department at the University of California, Berkeley. The faculty included, among others, Peter Voulkos, Don Potts, Mary Dumas, Willard Rosenquist, and, of course, Ed Rossbach, all of whom in their own ways were breaking the traditional boundaries of their respective mediums. Ed Rossbach, having been at the University from the early 1950s, was a seminal force in the contemporary fiber explorations. His influence as a teacher, artist and writer went far beyond the territory of his own immediate surroundings and students.

Unfortunately, the Design Department, as I had known it, no longer exists, and the important role it played in the lives of many artists and teachers is not well known and certainly not documented. Ed Rossbach was a major figure responsible for shaping the expansion and vision of the Design Department in the 1950s and 1960s, and his contribution to both the vitality of that department and the fiber movement should be recognized and acknowledged.

My first contact with Ed Rossbach came, indirectly, in the late 1960s. I had studied at the University of California, Berkeley, in the early 1960s, taking courses in art, ceramics and political science. Later, I studied weaving in Sweden for a year and returned to the Bay Area with an extensive technical knowledge of traditional weaving, determined to develop an art expression for myself that was textile-based but contemporary in nature. Aware of the contribution Voulkos was making in the field of ceramics, I was only vaguely familiar with Rossbach's contributions to contemporary fiber arts. I took summer classes in textiles at U.C. and joined a group of former students of Ed Rossbach's who met monthly to share slides, information and new ideas on the subject of textiles. The setting was Berkeley in the late 60s: we had been through anti-war protests, the free speech movement, the civil rights' movement, the women's movement, and the back-to-the-earth movement. Conditions were ripe for creative expression and for breaking boundaries. Rebelliousness and defiance were in the air.

Part of throwing off restrictions was also throwing off conventions of what was acceptable in art. We had Funk Art and Happenings. The atmosphere advocated the thinking that anything goes and everything be challenged: materials, processes, political comments on society and traditional art values. These were remarkable times, not only for the arts in general, but particularly for those artists expressing themselves in what traditionally had become known as the "Craft Media." Our group was built around a passionate interest in textiles—ethnographic, historic and contemporary— and a desire to share everything—slides, exhibitions, our travels, materials, ideas and trust. Nothing was held back for fear of one's losing while another gained, or of one's gaining at the expense of another. In this synergistic group we were all able to grow individually more than we could have alone. In part, all this activity must have been in keeping with the spirit of the place and the times, but the real catalyst seemed to be Rossbach. "I believe in being absolutely open and that the student could feel they could ask anything . . . and almost anything I would answer," he said, "and certainly I wouldn't have any secrets

76. **Toftner Square,** 1980
   Commercial cotton fabric, felt pen
   Silk screened, heat transfer printed, drawn
   89 1/2″ x 42″
   Collection of the Artist

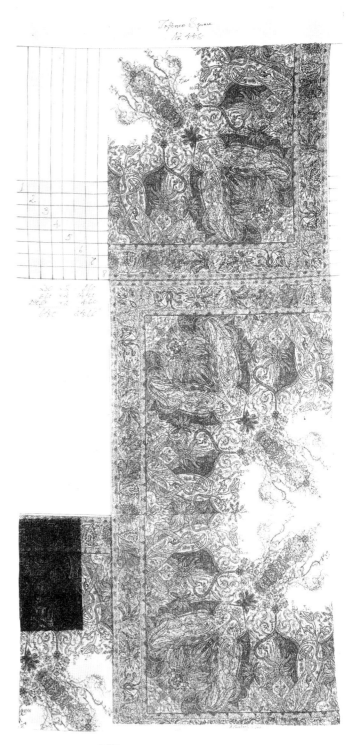

A
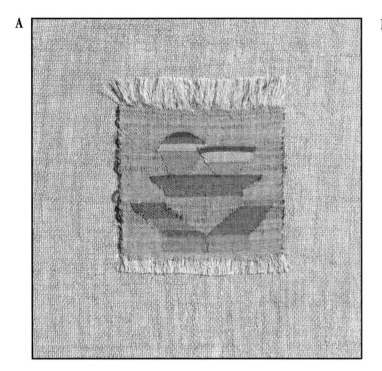

B

F

G
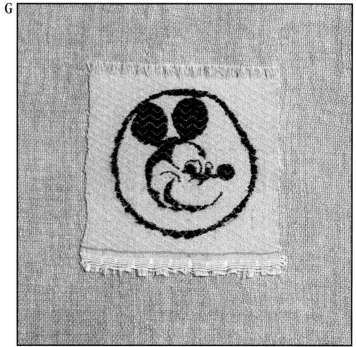

108

E

C

D

H

I

109

about my own work or how I did anything . . . This openness I valued very much." [1] It was against this backdrop that I went to graduate school.

Working under Rossbach I felt a great sense of freedom. It was a good program for someone who knew what she wanted and was self motivated. There were not the constraints that I have seen teaching in an art school, the abundance of reviews and evaluations, critiques held to make sure the student is doing well, that his/her work is developed sufficiently to "make it," to get the degree. In my own school experience there had been nothing of that at all. In fact, I don't even remember a formal critique session, ever. Yet I have never seen students work so hard or challenge themselves so much as we did. What was it then that worked so well for us? What was there in Ed Rossbach's teaching that inspired so many to go on to do such extraordinary and innovative things in their own right? Why have so many continued to cultivate a pas-

previous pages, from left:

77. **Brocaded Silks,** 1976
      Silk
      Twill weave, brocaded
      5" x 6" each

      a. **Homage to Boris Kroll**

      b. **18th Century Floral**

      c. **Spot II**

      d. **Katherine and Tyrone**

      e. **Cranes Fly**

      f. **Katherine and Tyrone II**

      g. **Mickey Mouse**

      h. **Mad Ludwig**

      i. **Mad Ludwig II**

      Collection of A. Sarazin, Milwaukee, Wisconsin
      Photo: Richard Eells

sion for textiles and the history of textiles long after its immediate popularity was over? I believe it was trust and respect for the individual as a creative being that provided the real basis for the successful working relationship with Rossbach and the impetus to continue experimenting.

Against this backdrop of trust and respect, everything was thrown back on the individual to decide. There was not a right or wrong, a good or bad. Doing anything in reaction to Rossbach was difficult because you never knew where you stood. I never knew exactly what he thought. Yet not knowing suited my way of working quite well. I became my own critic.

It's not that Rossbach didn't have strong ideas or opinions; he certainly did, but he was willing to step out of the way to allow each person to grow in his/her own unique way. Rossbach had a non-authoritarian approach. He simply trusted that the students when left to their own devices could and would produce something wonderful. "From the very beginning of my teaching I was absolutely delighted and enthralled by the creative work that my students did . . . The wonder—the infinite wonder—of the creative potential always stunned me. I often valued what my students did more than they did themselves." [2] Belief in the student's ability provided motivation and set the stage for a mutuality of trust. We knew something interesting would happen from listening to his musings, and he knew we would come up with something interesting as a result, and, finally, we too learned to trust in ourselves even more. It was an atmosphere of trust that went many ways. I believe that in this kind of atmosphere, when encouraged and stimulated, then left alone, students will do their best work. Whether the students do or don't, it is the process of becoming that is more important than measuring the progress.

Rossbach often shared with us a way of seeing. He would bring to class a bag or box with some objects.

Pulling from this bag something seemingly common but unusual, an old piece of textile, a plastic vegetable basket, he would share what he was thinking about when he saw this object, what it had reminded him of, how he had responded, and the questions that had come to mind. What he said and saw were often something unexpected. He wanted to know what we thought. His own perceptions were particularly personal. He showed us in a quiet, unassuming way where the "art idea" came from, how to look, how to see, and how to question and how to follow our own curiosity. We had fun. We would find ourselves, at that time, energized and spirited in each act of looking, seeing and doing. At that time, we didn't question how or why he did this, his philosophy of teaching. It worked, and the best evidence of its working lay in each of our individual doing.

Later, after many of us had become teachers ourselves, we tried to understand how he was able to **get** students to work, produce and develop in what seemed like such an effortless way. Maybe it was the times? Maybe we were exceptional students? Maybe it was Rossbach himself, his unique personality. Maybe all these things were true and maybe not. But finally, I feel that the essence of Rossbach's success was that he treated each student as an individual with trust and respect, and that set the stage for him to communicate his ideas in a very authentic, open manner. In this way, he communicated his interest in textiles as an expressive form, in art in the contemporary context, and in travel and non-Western sources of inspiration. He helped us to perceive what was around us,

78. **John Travolta,** 1978
Reeds, cotton twine, silk organza, electrical tape
Tied, heat transfer printed
17″ x 9″ x 7″
Collection of the Artist

111

79. **Purple Box,** 1985
   Ash splints, commercial fabric,
     newspaper, acrylic paint
   Plaited
   9″ x 11 1/2″ x 7 1/2″
   Collection of the Artist

80. **Lettuce Basket,** 1982
   Rice paper, newspaper,
     lacquer
   Plaited
   10″ x 9″ x 9″
   Collection of Dr. and Mrs.
     Milton Dalitzky, Long-
     meadow, Massachusetts

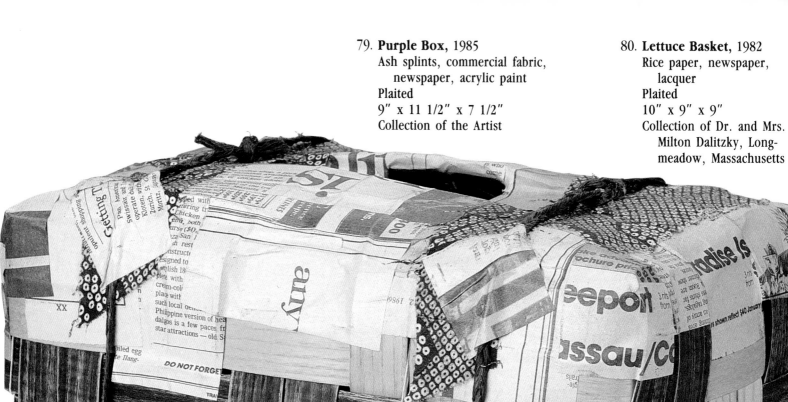

to rediscover the old in a new way, and to find value in things that others might regard as valueless.[3]

Though there was a great sense of freedom, there were also great expectations. Ed Rossbach expected a great deal from his students. However, it wasn't always clear exactly what those expectations were. Perhaps he didn't know himself. In any case, he wasn't going to tell us. That was something else we would have to figure out for ourselves. Always with the sense of expectation came a great deal of support. He writes about helping young people as he had been helped by a high school teacher of his, Edith Blaisdell Murphy: "I never thought about doing something to help other young people as she [Mrs. Murphy] did. I think any feelings that I have had about 'doing this for other young people' came later in my teaching. I felt it especially with my graduate students. . . . They came to seem so remarkable to me. I was enthralled by what they did, their originality and dedication and independence—and so on. They emerged, for me, as such strong individuals. Having contact with them enriched my life. I tried to let them know how valuable they were."[4]

I have come to the conclusion that Rossbach's success as a teacher was not something he just did or came by automatically; it was rather a refusal to be authoritarian and a conscious decision on his part to teach in a way that would bring out the most in the students, to nurture and not get in the way of their creativity. "I feel that about students, that they have these potentials, and I didn't even feel finally that I was directing them toward fulfilling their potential. I was just allowing them to—trying to make an environment . . . so that it would be possible for them to accept what they were doing. So that I accepted it, uncritically mainly."[5]

Ed Rossbach has had a profound influence on my life, my work and my teaching. Sometimes it is hard to know how much is a direct influence and how much is shared attitudes and values.

Clearly, Rossbach's lifestyle, combining the teaching of art with being an active practicing artist, has served as a model for my own. I have retained a commitment to exploring textiles as my primary medium, and use that medium as a means of expressing my ideas about contemporary art and life. Perhaps, though, the most significant influence Rossbach has exerted over me has been in terms of attitude. It is an attitude toward myself as an artist, an openness to what is there, to sharing with other artists and recognizing that we all build on one another. An attitude that welcomes risk-taking and encourages exploration and discovery. Here, the emphasis is on the activity, a process of art-making itself rather than on the production of a consistent body of work.

In the area of teaching, Rossbach has challenged me to create a demanding but open and accepting atmosphere. Like Rossbach, I try to treat my students as unique individuals who bear their own responsibility for the direction of their work. I try to emphasize what is strong or positive, to come from a position of trust that within a minimum of external controls, the students can use their own internal mechanism for change and growth. I try to communicate my love and passion for what I am doing so that the students can know something of what it is like to have an active life involved in the process of artmaking. I had thrived on the open and supportive atmosphere which empowered me to develop more of my own potential than I ever had before. As a teacher, I wish to pass on this experience.

Ed Rossbach, as a teacher, has profoundly influenced the lives, careers, and teaching of many other active artists as well. The students who have studied with him have gone on to embrace a wide range of activities and professions, everything from being museum curators, practicing artists and teachers, to doing research, designing or styling for industry.

That he stimulated students to follow their own unique direction underscores his support for each person as an individual. That his students remember so vividly his support underscores their respect for him as an educator. Pat Hickman spoke for many other former students like herself when she singled out for praise Rossbach's "belief in our ability to live up to our own potential" and his efforts to help students to discover their particular strengths.[6] On the other hand, each former student emphasized as well something slightly different about his or her experience with Rossbach. Katy Webb spoke of his "playful approach to thinking about things differently."[7] Pat Hickman gained a love of textile history through Rossbach and went on to teach textile history in addition to continuing her own work as an artist.[8] Chere Lai Mah emphasized his receptive quality: "He was like a space, a very empty space. I would go into his office and feel the silence. We would sit at his feet and he would tell us the most wonderful stories."[9] Lisa Lee Peterson spoke of Rossbach's "allowing space to be who we were," and found later in her own teaching that the "less I say the better they do," which she added, "works only if you are very strong."[10] Gyongy Laky particularly appreciated Rossbach's "fresh point of view." He was "very interested in his subject matter and daily discovered new things." His emphasis on cultures outside of the Western Art History tradition and his encouragement to go back to original sources eventually led her to spend a year in India exploring textiles.[11]

Rossbach the educator has touched the lives of people who have never been a student in his classes or who have never even met him personally. Those relationships have been built on what his many writings and lectures have communicated. John McQueen was deeply affected by Rossbach's book *Baskets as Textile Arts,* which opened his eyes to "aesthetic and philosophical" ideas about baskets.[12] "It was incredi-

ble to me that someone could write a book like that," he exclaimed in 1979.[13] More recently McQueen described the extent of Rossbach's continuing influence on his work: "I think of him as my mentor even though I have really only met him for a few minutes."[14]

With the current attitudes toward education I see today, which seem to stress practicality and financial security over risk-taking, I wonder how or if Ed Rossbach's approach to teaching would be influenced or altered in any way. I would prefer to think of Rossbach's teaching philosophy as a possible antidote to some of the pressures of our time. The shrinking housing market and the worry of students over future income and future lifestyles—create a student population that is too often interested in professionalism, profit, making it, rather than in artmaking as an intrinsically and personally valuable process. Rossbach's point of view, although not so popular at the moment, seems to offer the best possibility of liberation from some of these stresses and, ironically, a back door way of developing some of the most adventuresome, thought-provoking and uniquely personal art. In his own words, Rossbach leads us to a way of beginning:

> With students . . . I always wanted to say, "Trust me. Don't resist. Don't force me to beat my poor splendid wings trying to persuade you to something that you have set your mind against. Just go along, feel something, and let something happen."[15]

ROSSBACH IN CONTEXT
Nancy A. Corwin and Rebecca A.T. Stevens

The world of the textile artist in 1990 is far different than it was when Ed Rossbach graduated from Cranbrook with an MFA in ceramics and weaving in 1947. At that time the predominant aesthetic was Scandinavian Modern, textiles were for use, and most fiber artists designed for industry. Since that time textiles, as part of the post World War II crafts revival, have become an experimental, non-functional, expressive artistic medium and Ed Rossbach is one of the key figures to have shaped these changes. His "understanding of creativity and its relationship to craft has helped bring about the merging of art and craft."[1]

Although some fiber artists today are still employed as industrial designers, most work as independent artist/craftsmen and influence industrial design only indirectly. Many of these artists create for the limited production market selling their work in craft shops or at craft fairs. Others, however, utilize fibers to make art statements that parallel the current contemporary art movements in all media. It is the latter group that has been profoundly influenced by the work of Ed Rossbach. The aim of this essay is to place Rossbach's work in the evolving historical context of the fiber, craft and art worlds, and to describe his role as both an innovator and a participant in the post-war craft revival.

Rossbach is a rebel, a quiet revolutionary with a passionate curiosity and a wonderfully wry sense of humor. The breadth of his interests is extraordinary. He is one of a small number of artists who began in the 1950s to explore fibers as raw material for self-expression. Through his teaching, his research and writing, and his art, he has opened new avenues of expression and new ways of thinking that have changed forever the ways in which textiles are considered. He has opened minds with his work and has caused us to see textiles in a new way. Often that new way of seeing is accomplished through startling changes in scale or context, or ironic juxtapositions of materials and forms. In his use of changes in context and ironic contrasts, Rossbach has been the Marcel Duchamp of the textile world.

Rossbach has led the way in the exploration of textile structures, new materials and imagery, basketry as an expressive form, and, along with his wife, Katherine Westphal, photo processes in textile art. Rossbach's explorations have been remarkably parallel to the free experimentation of Abstract Expressionism, the irony of Pop and Funk Art, and the cerebral qualities of abstraction, Op Art and late 60s minimalist systems art.

He took fiber off the wall and made objects before object-making became a popular trend. He made "art about art" when that was a potent new form. He was interested in folk art in the early 1960s before its recent popularity.[2] In each of these explorations Rossbach was not concerned with following the latest

81. **Origami Basket with Mickey Mouse,** before 1981
New Zealand flax, rice paper, paint
Folded, tied
9 1/2" x 9 1/2" x 9"
Donna and William Nussbaum
Photo: Mark Katzman

trend in modern art. To the contrary, he has been consistently on the leading edge of art in his time following his own vision.

Rossbach continues to be part of the crafts revival movement and a formative figure in it. Yet he has not been a rural Thoreau figure like many of the early crafts revival pioneers. He has lived and taught in Berkeley, a sophisticated academic community which was a center of agitation during the turbulent years of the 1960s. This complex milieu is reflected in his work.

In the discussion that follows, we have deliberately used long quotes from Ed Rossbach's many written replies and oral interviews. He is an eloquent writer who sees his writing as part of his creative work, so we are letting him speak for himself wherever possible.

1940s: THE FOUNDATIONS

Rossbach's early art training was in painting and design. His most important undergraduate teachers at the University of Washington were European emigres who were dedicated to a new approach to the making of art. Both Johannes Molzahn, who had been a teacher at the German Bauhaus, and Amedee Ozenfant, who along with Le Corbusier had been one of the leading theorists and founders of French Purism, advocated a "machine aesthetic" in which painting and design were to evoke a rational, mathematical sense of order. The artist's expressive vocabulary was to include only the primary elements of color, line and form which were viewed as culturally non-specific, therefore, "pure art." These formal elements were intended to appeal to the intellectual side of man and were thought to be more valid than the subjective emotional approach of past art. The mathematical sense of order inherent in weaving and other textile structures utilized by Rossbach is consistent with the aims of Molzahn and Ozenfant. The philosophy of his early

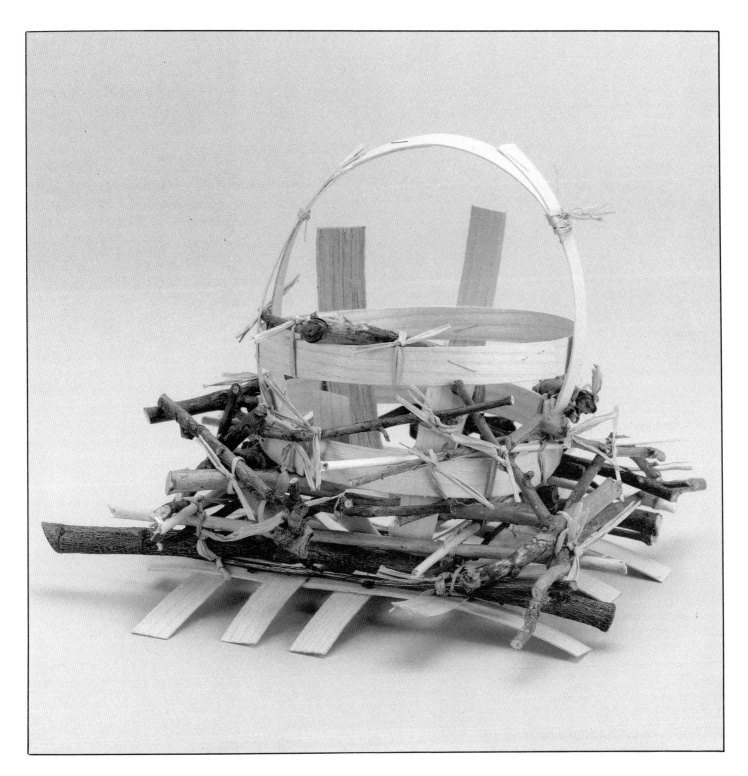

118

teachers must certainly have played a role in his ultimate choice of medium, although his work evolved in expressive and pictorial ways never advocated by them. According to Rossbach:

> When I was a student at the University of Washington I studied with a painter—one of the degenerate artists who was obliged to flee Germany—who greatly influenced me and my work. He took art seriously in a way unlike anyone whom I had ever come in contact with . . . Anyway, I had saved some exercises that I did in Molzahn's class. They were student works, on cheap paper, and had become brittle and yellow. After I had visited the Bauhaus Archives Museum in West Berlin, it occurred to me that these exercises might be of interest to the Archives as representatives of what influence Molzahn had exerted in the United States. The Archives were pleased to have them, and wrote me some time later to tell me that they had been on exhibit for awhile in the Bauhaus museum. This is not to suggest that I was 100% involved in what Molzahn was teaching.[3]

Neither did Rossbach remain completely involved in Ozenfant's philosophy: "Once I was away from his classes, I reacted against what he was teaching—his approach—the cool, intellectual refinement of everything."[4] However, Rossbach accepted one of Ozenfant's basic tenets as his own most productive method of creating art. Ozenfant is credited with being the first of the modern art theorists to emphasize the importance of creating art in a progressive series of works. Ozenfant felt that in taking one idea and exploring it in a logical progression from one piece to

82. **Small Basket of Splints, Twigs,** 1984
   Twigs, ash splints, raffia
   Plaited, tied, stapled
   8 1/2″ x 9 1/2″ x 10″
   Collection of the Artist

the next, artists were able to refine their ideas.[5] Rossbach has created art in this way throughout his career, often picking up where he left off on a direction after a long interruption. (See Rowe's discussion.)

Two central, but sometimes contradictory, ingredients of Rossbach's art background have been structure and abstraction on the one hand and expressionism on the other. His career shows a lifelong concern with balancing or integrating these apparently contradictory qualities. Thus, by 1948, partly as a reaction to the formalism of Ozenfant, Rossbach's favorite painter was the German Expressionist Max Beckmann, who had just immigrated to the United States:

> I think that the exhibit that had the most impact when I was in college was the show of paintings by Max Beckmann. I wrote to the dealer to find out how much a painting cost. I had fantasies about buying one—when I was scrounging along on a shoestring. And I wonder what my life would have been had I been able to buy one of those paintings. . . . I think I responded to the same qualities in Goya that I responded to in the paintings of Max Beckmann. The intensity, the emotional quality.[6]

Rossbach's simultaneous fascination with the contradictory qualities of reason and emotion is also reflected in the playful, humorous or startling ways he presents his scholarly investigation of textile structures. In this way he makes the technical insights more accessible.

During his student years in the 1940s, the major influences on textiles, ceramics and interior decoration in the United States were Bauhaus and Scandinavian Design; Bauhaus ideas were predominant. Initially the Bauhaus produced a few experimental weavings, some of which were pictorial, but after 1925 Bauhaus' emphasis in fiber, as in all craft media, shifted firmly to functionalism and the formal properties of art. Although some American artists before the 1940s, such

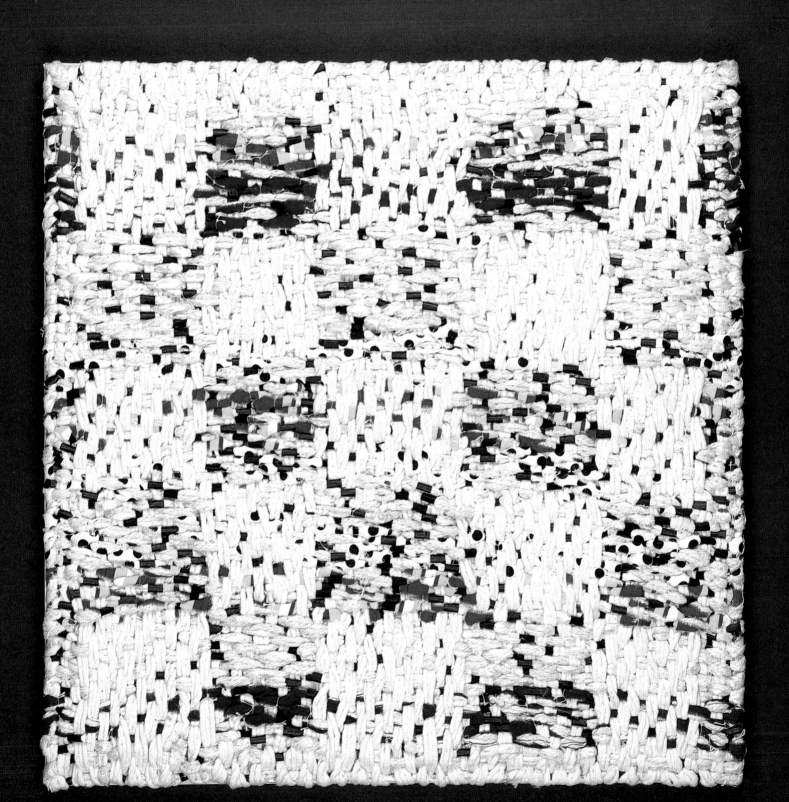

as Marguerite Zorach, had explored fibers as a medium of artistic expression, such artists remained isolated. The mainstream viewpoint established by the many Bauhaus instructors who immigrated to the United States was that textiles should be governed by functionalism and formal design elements.

Anni Albers, the foremost Bauhaus weaver to have settled in the United States, exemplified that formalism and concern with function. While teaching at Black Mountain College from 1933 to 1949, she experimented with texture, structure, and synthetic materials such as rayon and cellophane, within the confines of functional fabrics. Only after she left Black Mountain, did she begin to concentrate on her expressive weavings.[7] Although she had no direct followers, her influence, primarily through her writings, on Rossbach and all fiber artists prior to 1950 was inescapable. Throughout his life Rossbach has maintained a strong interest both in the formal characteristics of fiber art and in experimentation with unconventional materials. He retains an admiration for the Bauhaus teachers and their role in history.[8]

The Bauhaus had a profound influence in the United States, where the prosperous Post World War II economy offered fertile ground to cultivate the optimistic goal of good design (and a better life) for all citizens. In this respect the Bauhaus attempted to take the ideas of William Morris, father of the Arts and Crafts Movement, and integrate them with the new industrial society: the goal was to combine "the sensibilities of the artist" and "the knowledge of the technician to create new forms in architecture and de-

83. **Damask Waterfall,** 1977
Cotton welting cord, commercial fabric, plastic
Satin damask, wrapped
36" x 36"
Collection of the Artist

sign."[9] The Bauhaus sought to educate a generation of artists who would work for the industries which provided affordable goods to ordinary citizens (unlike the high priced handcrafts of the Arts and Crafts Movement). These artists were to use knowledge of materials and handcraft processes to create good design. Walter Gropius, founding director, clearly stated these aims in the manifesto at the opening of the school in 1919: "The artist is an exalted craftsman . . . *proficiency in his craft is essential to every artist. Therein lies the source of creative imagination.*"[10]

How closely Rossbach's early thinking echoed Gropius' ideas is apparent in a 1948 article he wrote for *Craft Horizons.* "The handweaver who would keep his craft a vital and significant art form must be thoroughly familiar with the medium." He went on to say that the handweaver should have an important artistic statement to make and should continually explore the medium for the most effective means of expressing his ideas.[11]

Cranbrook Academy of Art, where Rossbach studied for his MFA in 1946 and 1947, promoted the ideals of the Bauhaus and the Arts and Crafts Movement in the United States in a slightly different form. There the teachers were Scandinavian not German. Scandinavian weaving was the dominant style at Cranbrook, and it played an important role in the development of weaving in United States during the 40s and 50s, a role which has never really been assessed, according to Rossbach: "The Scandinavian women had skill and real influence when they came here . . . look at 1940s weaving and there's a clear connection with Scandinavian folk weaving."[12] Of his years at Cranbrook, Rossbach said,

> At the time I went to Cranbrook—everything has changed since then—the approach to textiles was extremely narrow, with strict limitations on what the students were allowed to weave. By the time I left, I was already ran-

kling under this approach, although I had no idea what I thought textile education should, or could, be. The approach at Cranbrook seemed a dead end . . . We wove some beautiful lengths within these restrictions—they all said 'contemporary weaving' loud and clear, and they were technically competent and in good taste. Mild good taste.[13]

Marianne Strengell, his teacher, hired in 1937 from Sweden, evidently never emphasized the 500 piece textile study collection that had been donated by Cranbrook's founder. According to Rossbach, she exposed her students to no other weaving than the Cranbrook method, which was based on Scandinavian weaving and allowed only flossa rugs and plain, twill and tapestry weaves.[14] As a result his knowledge of textile structures was limited:

> When I left Cranbrook and bought a loom of my own I bought a Cranbrook loom, since it was really the only loom I knew anything about. I immediately started breaking away although I had no clear idea of what I wanted to do, or what the possibilities were. Cranbrook provided me with a foundation from which I could take off. Yet the only realization of the wonder of textiles came from Maija Grotell, the teacher of ceramics. She discussed my textiles with me and showed me textiles that she had brought with her from Finland. Her response to textiles was so emotional, and so sensitive—it put textiles into another realm of meaning and expression.
> . . . The textile studio was all concerned with production and, somehow, 'success.' The ceramic studio for me was emotion and feeling.[15]

Here again we have that dichotomy of reason and emotion in Rossbach's life, and his attempt to balance and integrate the two forces. Although very much attracted to the emotive quality in painting, Rossbach has been more reserved in his textile work:

> I felt that I censored my work. Which, of course, I still do. I think I have pretty much steered clear of a big emotional emphasis in my textile work, partly because the scene is not accepting, but also because of my own reticence.[16]

Yet another carryover from Cranbrook days, his choice of materials, affected Rossbach's later work greatly. At Cranbrook he had had to "scrounge" for supplies because of shortages after the war, so he became accustomed to using ordinary string, rope, twine, plastic, and paper. In order to secure more traditional materials he had to plan far in advance, thus inhibiting his spontaneity. He attributes his interest in unconventional media to that time, but points out that he identifies as much with fine silk as with those materials. He liked the extremes; at the same time that he was using everyday plastics he was using very beautiful silks.[17]

1950S: ROSSBACH MATURES AS AN ARTIST

During his first teaching post at the University of Washington, Rossbach began to study those textile structures such as doublecloth which were previously unknown to him. (See Doublecloth Fabric, 1949, Fig. 2) The move from Seattle in 1950 to teach at the University of California at Berkeley was the catalyst for entering a period of growth and experimentation. He was influenced by the Berkeley curriculum and collections and by developments in ceramics and current art movements like Abstract Expressionism.

Berkeley was the first university department to offer a masters degree in weaving.[18] It had a well-developed curriculum on which Rossbach built a dynamic program. He attracted a committed group of talented students in the 60s and 70s whom he enjoyed immensely and who were strongly influenced by him.

The teaching at Berkeley was based on theory and practice with each studio course matched by a textile

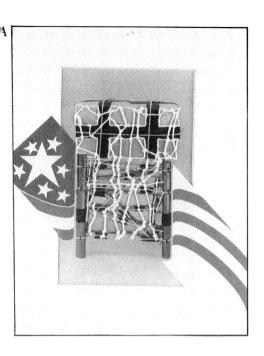

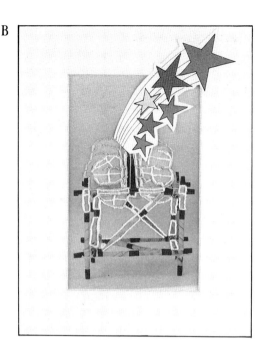

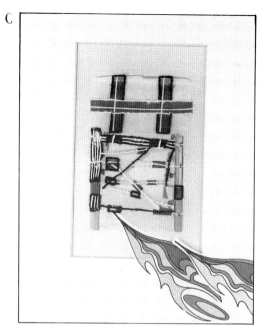

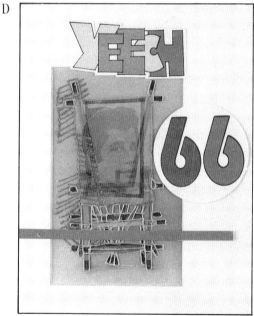

history course which used the departmental and Museum of Anthropology collections as examples. Rossbach immersed himself in historical textiles, particularly those of ancient pre-industrial cultures. Beyond the departmental requirements, he felt an obligation to himself as a creative artist and to his students to understand thoroughly what he was teaching.[19] The most heavily utilized textiles were those of pre-Spanish peoples of Peru. Many were made on simple looms which allowed the weaver to introduce intricate hand techniques long forgotten by modern weavers. Still other Peruvian textiles were not made on looms at all, but by the direct manipulation of fibers by hand. These textiles were to have a significant influence on Rossbach, and, beyond him, on the field as a whole, for if textiles of both the industrial and fine art areas were to develop, they had to go beyond the narrow confines of European traditions. Rossbach realized this need to expand horizons and, as a result, began to include in his life extensive travel to study textiles in their original contexts. (See Brite/Caldwell discussion.)

These ancient textile ideas were profoundly liberating for the few weavers like Rossbach, Sheila Hicks, and Lenore Tawney who began to investigate them in the 1950s. Rossbach was fortunate in that no other

84. **Postcards,** 1976
   a. **Stars and Stripes**
   b. **Star Wars**
   c. **Jet Propelled**
   d. **John Travolta**
   Paper, cotton thread, commercial decals from cereal box
   Photographed, glued, embroidered, painted
   9 1/2" x 7 1/2" each
   Collection of the Artist

123

textile department in the country could boast such a distinguished study collection, not even Cranbrook. The impetus these textiles gave him and a whole generation of his students to explore the expressive possibilities of fibers cannot be overestimated, especially in the 1960s when artists began to abandon the inflexibility of loom-controlled structures.

A structure Rossbach explored briefly in the early 1950s was gauze weave. In preparation for his teaching, Lea Miller gave him Lila O'Neale's book on gauze weaves and he did a reconstruction. (See Rowe discussion.) Miller was particularly interested in gauzes then, doing them on a loom with doup heddles. Rossbach, fascinated by them in a completely different way, was content to do them on a loom with hand pickup. Miller was also using plastics at that time and gave some to Rossbach which he wove into gauze weave. There were also essential differences in their uses of plastics: Miller used them in a very elegant, refined way, whereas Rossbach liked ordinary plastic, he says, "as it came off a loaf of bread."[20]

Rossbach became interested in ikats in the 1950s as a result of his teaching. No contemporary Americans were weaving ikats at that time. Rossbach's method of working was highly experimental, mixing techniques in unorthodox ways. He felt that the liquid colors and shifting patterns of ikats provided an expressive, painterly avenue for the making of textiles. Just as he had done earlier with **Tule Screen,** 1954 (Fig. 7), in which he used soft, spongy, subtle-colored materials, he sought to break out of the right-angle rigidity of his earlier textile training. **Double Ikat,** 1956 (Fig. 14), is an example of his painterly approach to the patterning of textiles.

The 1950s marked a time of change in all art media and California was an important source of that artistic fermentation. Abstract Expressionist painting, advocating the spontaneous and expressive uses of materials and processes, was by then an international movement that had reached San Francisco. This was a heady, energetic time of post World War II prosperity and expansion which affected the universities. Rossbach's gradual move into more expressive work was part of these larger art world developments which opened up attitudes in all areas. The exuberant, rebellious confidence of the 1950s can still be sensed from reading the works of Jack Kerouac and other beat writers who congregated in Northern California.[21]

Ceramics, the first craft medium to change, paved the way for new developments in fiber art. Ceramics in the 50s was influenced by both the Japanese folk aesthetic and Abstract Expressionist painting; each emphasized freedom and natural, expressive use of materials and process. These qualities gradually replaced the cool precision and functionalism of the Scandinavian Modern aesthetic. Peter Voulkos was a key figure in bringing these two schools of thought to bear on the ceramic medium, through his interests in the ceramics of Picasso and Miro, jazz music, New York Expressionist painting, and the ideas of Japanese folk potters such as Shoji Hamada. By the time he came to teach at Berkeley in 1958-59, he was already breaking down the boundaries between functional ceramics and sculpture in his highly expressive work.

Ed Rossbach was interested in promoting experimentation with craft media, and in 1958, was instrumental in bringing Peter Voulkos to Berkeley to teach ceramics in the Decorative Art Department. He had seen Voulkos' earlier shows at California College of Arts and Crafts and Gumps, and admired his experimentalism. It was Rossbach who urged his hiring and who went to Los Angeles to invite Voulkos to Berkeley. Rossbach points out how important Voulkos was to the whole craft movement: "He was so daring."[22] Rossbach was beginning to be daring as well. In **Printed Textile,** 1959 (Fig. 22), he drew on the cloth with felt markers, and in **Reconstituted Commercial Textile, 1960** (Fig. 23), he encased the fabric in plastic tubing.

Ceramics with its powerful, even flamboyant, personalities, was crucial to the recognition of other crafts materials as legitimate materials for artistic expression. The more aggressive parts of the clay world wanted to "make it" in the art world and were at odds with much of the craft world's rejection of the art market's hype. There are still two views and many variants within the craft movement. Rossbach is more sympathetic to those who shy away from dramatic art market publicity.

During the 1950s Rossbach's work was also strongly influenced by ethnic textiles and the design world. **African Reeds,** 1952 (Fig. 12), reflects his interest in weaving with slats and other alternative types of wefts and was partly influenced by the slat screens of Dorothy Liebes. **Ikat** and **Double Ikat** of 1956 (Figs. 13 & 14), reflect experiments in connection with his teaching, long before the great popularity of ikat in the 1970s. **Printed Textile,** 1959 (Fig. 22), is stencil resist dyed, a technique used in Japan and elsewhere. These and the two African raffia pieces, **African Congo Weavings I and II** of 1952 (Figs. 4 & 5), were highly experimental but still were flat two-dimensional wall pieces. Fiber had not yet come "off the wall," but then neither had most paintings. Robert Rauschenberg, whose early combines were not produced until the mid 50s, led the way.[23]

The two raffia panels mentioned above, woven shortly after Rossbach came to Berkeley (see Rowe discussion), illustrate the inspiration he derived from the study collections, and his openness to cross-cultural

approaches in art. In his hands traditional rules were abandoned: African weavings were woven and manipulated on a western loom for different effects. The innovative use of traditional forms and the startling departure from convention are the keys to Rossbach's art, writing and teaching. He turns the rules upside down, and that accounts for his impact on the world of textile arts.

85. **Homage to Richard Wagner,** 1985
Ash splints, rice paper, lacquer
Plaited, heat transfer printed
13″ x 9″ x 9″
Dr. and Mrs. Edward Okun
Photo: Ft. Wayne Indiana Museum of Art

The impact was felt gradually in the 50s but much more significantly in the 60s and 70s. Simplicity and complexity were balanced and played off against each other. We sense in his concentration on textile structures an almost spiritual nostalgia for the perfection that Bauhaus design and early 20th century abstract painting tried to attain with their reductiveness:

> I used often to think how satisfying it would be to weave just plain weave, with the same warp as weft, perfectly spaced in a square count. No color or fiber changes—just perfect structure. Of course, I never did it. Once at a state fair I judged the weavings. One was a perfect balance of warp and weft which was unbelievably satisfying. I have always remembered it. I gave it a second prize. I hadn't the absolute confidence in my feelings to give it first place over something more imaginative or 'creative' (which I have completely forgotten). When I see minimal paintings—an entire canvas painted solid blue, for instance, saying 'blue,' I think of wanting perfect structure, no more, no less.[24]

Rossbach's interest in geometric systems of structures in the 1960s and later parallels the interests of some Minimalist artists such as Sol Lewitt and Agnes Martin.[25] He is aware that in textile structures there are the same grids, the same geometric harmonies. Mondrian, Molzahn and other such reductive abstrac-

tionists of the early twentieth century were their precursors in this search for cosmic order. These ideas are central to Rossbach's work and his contribution to the craft revial. Rossbach describes how he likes to look at books with diagrams of historic techniques because he "likes to see how the threads work."[26] He wants others to see how the threads work as well. One way he highlighted structure was to enlarge dramatically its scale. Another was to use unexpected materials which arrest the viewer's attention. **Construction with Newpapers and Plastic,** 1968 (Fig. 38), is an example of his use of both devices.

Rossbach's transition from functional textiles of the 40s to the art fabrics of the 60s was not abrupt. It was a gradual change in which he wove theoretically utilitarian fabrics (although he never marketed them) while also experimenting with the expressive qualities of textiles as art. He and his wife, Katherine, produced surface designs for textiles in the 1950s, which were sold to textile manufacturers through their New York agent, Frederick Karoly. Rossbach said he enjoyed making the designs and found the experience "very rewarding" at the time.[27]

During the same period, the striped ikat made in 1956 (Fig. 13) (discussed by Rowe), was finished. In it he intended to express through the pattern of the colors the two dimensions of time and space instead of the two dimensions of height and width. Rossbach says he was inspired by a dance composition not a visual pattern in making this piece. Another example, of his expresive use of the technique is **Double Ikat,** 1959 (Fig. 14). It was woven in the format of an industrial prototype but did not have the expected repeat pattern which would have made it producible. It needs to be seen in its entirety to be appreciated as an abstract color statement.

In 1960, he wove a linen and silk length (Fig. 19) now in the collection of the Art Institute of Chicago, which was admired by Jack Lenor Larsen and adapted

86. **El Salvador,** 1984
    Muslin, camouflage netting, sticks, plastic, plastic tape, wire
    Tied, dyed, linoleum block printed, constructed
    15 1/2″ x 15 1/2″ x 13″
    Collection of the Artist

87. **New World Egg,** 1985
    Ash splints, rice paper
    Plaited, heat transfer printed
    17″ x 15″ x 15″
    Collection of the Artist

by him for an industrially manufactured fabric called **Bamako,** 1962-3 (Fig. 18). However, yardage had ceased to hold Rossbach's attention. His work after 1962 makes it clear that the expressive qualities of textiles had become his predominant interest. His work, for example **Ceremonial Plate with Face,** 1965 (Fig. 28), attempts to look for the meaning of 20th century life in its common everyday objects. He interjects into a twentieth century container associations from history of ritual and commemorative functions, to give the object a spiritual, emotional content, such as was found in Renaissance ceramic birth platters or precious metalwork pattens from the Middle Ages. He sought to reinject the human element into what had become the non-human (i.e. machine made). He once wrote, "A special quality of a handwoven textile . . . is its ability to evoke an awareness that someone, someplace, wove it . . . the textile speaks not of a life, but life."[28] Rossbach wanted to speak of twentieth century life in his works.

1960s AND BEYOND: EXPERIMENTALISM

Raffia Panel, 1964 (Fig. 24), was selected along with the work of several other textile artists to represent the United States in the 13th Triennale di Milano, 1964, an international exposition which brought together the most innovative design work from all over the world.[29] Rossbach's piece was woven of natural raffia in a very laborious technique with discontinuous warps and wefts inspired by the pre-Spanish Peruvians. In Rossbach's truly contradictory fashion, it is a subtle study of texture, line and positive/negative space, meticulously fashioned in a material that paradoxically has no value in Western culture. The common material was purposefully chosen to diminish the importance of the medium and emphasize the formal design qualities of the work. To make the

piece, he actually had to counterbalance the physical pressure of forces pulling the raffia in different directions. Rossbach says the sense of equilibrium which he achieved in this piece recalls for him the paintings of Piet Mondrian which speak of visual equilibrium of intersecting forces. (See Rowe discussion.)

The piece also marks a direction Rossbach has continued to the present day in which he elects to "value the valueless," by using pedestrian materials like raffia, old newspapers, and plastic packing materials of our society for his personal expression. By his own admission, he retreats into the most devalued pursuits in order to survive with his values as intact as possible, where money and society's artificial status symbols have no meaning for him.[30] Rossbach's attitude echoes ideas of Marcel Duchamp whose art provoked renewed interest in the late 50s, and those of Robert Rauschenberg. In using found materials and, in Rauschenberg's case, photo images from everyday life, all sought to bridge the gap between art and life.[31]

At the time Rossbach completed his **Raffia Panel** in 1964, he was extremely interested in the textile fragments of past civilizations as cultural markers. In this particular piece he acknowledges his debt to the Peruvian people who taught him, through their textile artifacts, to appreciate their inventiveness and their sense of time, so unlike our own. The successful completion of their task of making the textile was paramount; the amount of time taken in its completion was unimportant. **Raffia Panel** is a personal artifact of a twentieth century man who can utilize the Peruvians and Mondrian as historical inspirations. Rossbach's attitudes anticipated those of process artists like Eva Hesse, whose work is about the making of the object rather than the finished objects themselves, and ritual object artists like Michelle Stuart, whose work explores the associations in objects, especially those from pre-industrial societies.

The 1960s witnessed a growth of interest in all

craft media. The Centre International de la Tapisserie Ancienne et Moderne, under the leadership of tapestry artist Jean Lurcat, organized the first of what became the most influential series of fiber exhibitions in the world. Originally conceived as a showcase for the revival of traditional woven tapestry, the *Biennale Internationale de la Tapisserie*, in Lausanne, Switzerland, soon evolved to include, by the third Biennale in 1967, "research without other [technique] stipulation."[32] The size requirement for entries also changed from a minimum of twelve square meters to a minimum of five square meters. Yet it was still the intention of the organizing committee to show only monumental works in the grand European tradition of Medieval and Renaissance tapestry production. Although much fiber art in the 60s and 70s, inspired in part by Abstract Expressionism, explored large scale, clearly not every artist working in textiles made pieces that would meet these requirements. Rossbach did not care to work large, and for that reason he never applied to exhibit in this prestigious series.

In order to complete works on that monumental scale, he would have needed to have worked with assistants, a concept totally alien to Ed Rossbach's private approach to art. He only once used an assistant, on **Log Cabin Sham,** 1967 (Fig. 44). After its completion he felt removed from the piece, from the process of making and the surprises and decisions that occur as a piece develops.[33] For these and other reasons, he has never done commissioned work either. Rossbach's influence has instead been disseminated by key exhibitions in the United States. His thinking has been car-

ried abroad through the work of the many artists who have studied with him, and who have exhibited in the *Biennales* and other important international exhibitions.

Exhibitions were especially significant in the 60s and 70s because their accompanying catalogs or poster announcements were the major way fiber artists remained in touch with what others in the field were doing.[34] The two landmark 1969 exhibitions, *Wall Hangings* at the Museum of Modern Art in New York, and *Objects: USA,* a touring exhibition which opened at the National Collection of Fine arts (now the National Museum of American Art) of the Smithsonian Institution), brought a wider appreciation of Rossbach's work.[35] Fiber art pioneer Claire Zeisler singles out the Museum of Modern Art exhibition as the opportunity for her first real appreciation of his work.[36] She was

following page:
89. **Eskimo Pie,** 1987
   Cardboard food carton, spray lacquer
   Folded, stapled
   7" x 7 1/2" x 7 1/2"
   Donna and William Nussbaum   88. **Ed with Sam,** 1985

Photo: Mark Katzman

130

entranced by his original use of throwaway materials in works such as **Construction with Newspaper and Plastic,** 1968 (Fig. 38). *Objects: USA* included his **Basket with Handle,** 1966 (Fig. 29), revealing to a wide audience his growing interest in basket structures which had begun a revolution in the making of baskets as textile art. His thinking was defined in writing with the publication of his first book on the subject in 1973, *Baskets as Textile Art.*

Rossbach has continued to exhibit since the 1960s but with little interest in showing his work in commercial galleries (the recent exceptions being Miller/Brown Gallery in San Francisco and Bellas Artes in Santa Fe) or in promoting his commercial career. Self-promotion and marketing are alien to Rossbach's nature and philosophy, and the art itself defies the conventional ideas of beauty, size and permanence of materials associated with the art market. This non-commercial stance has always been admired by his students as an authentic statement coming through in both his art and his life. In fact, he has spent so little time in these activities that when a gallery owner sold one of his favorite pieces, **Modular Construction,** 1968 (Fig. 46), in 1970, he never asked who bought it. He only discovered in a conversation while organizing this retrospective that the piece is now in the collection of the Milwaukee Art Museum. When the Musee des Arts Decoratifs de Montreal wanted two works, Rossbach gave them to the museum in 1985 as he has done for other institutions, instead of selling the pieces. Appreciation and understanding of his work and textiles in general are far more important to him than financial reward. As a result, he has never pursued public commissions, but has preferred to publicize his artistic ideas by writing. His extensive list of books and articles on both history and technique have been widely read and, in the case of his two books on basketry, have affected the course of fiber art in this country and abroad. It is generally acknowledged that

the contemporary basketry movement started with Ed Rossbach. Lillian Elliott points out that by the 12th *Biennale* (1985) in Lausanne, a number of works related to basketry, and these were not only by Americans.[37]

Rossbach's early experiments with baskets during the war when stationed in the Aleutian Islands had produced no results. His basketmaking really began in earnest in the 1960s when one of his students was doing research in baskets for special studies in anthropology and sparked his thinking about the relationship between hard and soft textiles.[38] The three baskets he exhibited at Museum West in 1965 and at the Museum of Contemporary Crafts in 1968, were among the first baskets he ever made, but even in these he was not following traditional methods. **Hornets' Nest,** 1964, (Fig. 26) from that period, was coiled but then rubbed with gesso to age the surface. **Looped Cylinder,** 1964 (Fig. 27), was made by looping—not a basketry method but a net or bagmaking technique. What is important even with these is his experimentation with materials and techniques and his disregard of traditional methods.

Rossbach has used an astonishing variety of techniques in his baskets over the past 25 years, ranging from plaiting with splints to lace techniques. The basket has been his main three-dimensional form of expression particularly since 1975. He began basketmaking in the 1960s, a time when the line between sculpture and painting was beginning to blurr, and artists were beginning to create mixed media objects. His interest in the vessel form was probably inspired by this coming together of sculpture and painting, but also by developments in ceramics in the Berkeley area where Peter Voulkos and Ron Nagle were making nonfunctional vessel forms. Nagle's cups were "in a sense not a cup, but about cups," and were often visual puns.[39] Voulkos' vessels were slashed open and painted, no longer functioning as containers.

Rossbach's baskets, like Voulkos' vessels, became potent three dimensional forms, communicating on many levels. Baskets are traditionally humble and anonymous functional objects used by the non-industrialized peoples of the world; Rossbach capitalizes on these associations and uses baskets additionally as sculpture, or as a carrier for images. By making baskets from non-traditional materials and placing on or in them political protest and social images from contemporary life, or by finishing them by simply stapling them, he creates contradictions which startle us into thinking about the paradoxes in our lives. In America today we have great wealth but waste so much. We throw away tons of newspaper and plastic in our society indiscriminately. Rossbach saves it and uses it meticulously. He shows us that this material can have beauty and value. Thus, Rossbach's art is simple and complex at the same time. Another layer of irony exists in such small and simple forms and techniques being used for complex images and meanings. He was surprised, he said, when **Beirut Basket,** a political protest, sold because he thought people didn't want baskets to carry images.[40] That, of course, is exactly why he uses imagery on baskets.

Like the Dada artists before him, Rossbach loves everyday found objects and materials like plastic and newspaper. The inspiration for using plastic dates from his Cranbrook days, the newspaper from the late 60s. He says of this choice of found materials:

> I just happen to like it (plastic), I guess partly because other people don't like it. In the textile field there are such romantic notions about spinning, wool, raising sheep, etc. It all becomes sort of homey, homely, homespun. . . . Plastic is not warm. It is not nice. It is not approved. It has no history. It is bad taste. It is a cheap substitute. It is garish. It is too shiny. I like it. . . . I love the ease of newspaper. . . . I am not trying to be ingenious or clever and trying to do the most far out thing that I can. . . .

> Or arrest your attention because it's different. . . . I like the idea that at the same time that I was working in newspaper I was working with the finest silk that I could get. I like the feeling that the extremes of—that I work in the extremes. . . . I like that contradictory sort of thing. I like doing things that I think could possibly last and things that obviously aren't going to last too long . . . extremes. Yes, I like to do things that are absolutely technically perfect and I like to do things that look as though a child made them.[41]

To understand this love of contradictions it is also important to view Rossbach's work not only in the context of Duchamp and Rauschenberg, but also in light of what was happening in San Francisco, where the cool Pop Art of New York was transformed into the hot, engaged Funk sculpture movement, mainly by clay artists of the 60s. Peter Selz describes the scene:

> Funk art, so prevalent in the San Francisco Bay Area is largely a matter of attitude. But many of the works also reveal certain similar characteristics of form—or anti-form. In the current spectrum of art, Funk is at the opposite extreme of such manifestations as New York 'primary structures' or the 'Fetish Finish' sculpture which prevails in Southern California. Funk art is hot rather than cool; it is committed rather than disengaged; it is bizarre rather than formal; it is

90. **Eagle's Nest Box,** 1984
Twigs, raffia, corrugated cardboard, newspaper, lacquer
Tied, constructed
15 1/2" x 16" x 16"
Collection of the Artist

91. **Fancy Plaid,** 1983
Ash splints, paper, commercial fabric, lacquer
Plaited
13" x 6" x 6"
Mr. and Mrs. Sanford M. Besser, Little Rock, Arkansas
Photo: Vince Foster

133

sensuous; and frequently it is quite ugly and un-gainly. Although usually three-dimensional, it is non-sculptural in any traditional way, and ir-reverent in attitude. It is symbolic in content and evocative in feeling. Like many contem-porary novels, films and plays, Funk art looks at things which traditionally were not meant to be looked at . . . like the dialogue in a play by Ionesco or Beckett, the juxtaposition of unex-pected things seems to make no apparent sense. Funk is visual talk, it makes fun of itself, although often (though by no means all the time) it is dead serious. Making allusions, the artist is able, once more, to deprecate himself with a true sense of the ironic.[42]

However, Rossbach's forms, his interplay and jux-taposition of materials and imagery were quieter, never brazenly sexual or vulgar like Funk. Rossbach says of a 1968 work, **Christmas Basket** (Fig. 54): ''I wanted to give it a title that would suggest that I meant it to be funky, but I couldn't think of a title and, to be perfectly honest, funk isn't my basket.''[43] ''Perhaps,'' as Selz says of the roots of Funk, ''again it is Marcel Duchamp's stance that is of the greatest importance here, his total absence of taste (good or bad) in the selection of his ready-mades, his indiffer-ence to form and indifference even to certain objects he created.''[44] For Rossbach form is often anti-form: humble, atypical, awkward, unbeautiful (**Lettuce Basket,** 1982 [Fig. 80]; **Buffalo Basket,** 1987 [Fig. 101]; or **Plastic Bag,** 1970 [Fig. 57]).

Rossbach's materials are often not meant to last. He recalls with amusement that once a gallery reimbursed him for a basket because while it was on exhibition it had been eaten by vermin.[45] His imagery, taken from popular culture, also celebrates the ephemeral. **John Travolta,** 1978 (Fig. 78), for example, represents a man who is no longer a current matinee idol. Mickey Mouse, at first glance a cool pop image, embodies, in truth, an ironic twist and comment on contemporary

attitudes. (See **Mickey Mouse Lace,** 1971 [Fig. 72]; **Minnie Mouse,** 1975 [Fig. 70]; **Mickey Mouse Coil Basket,** 1975 [Fig. 73]; **Mickey Mouse Brocade,** 1976 [Fig. 77]; **Damask Mickey Mouse,** 1976 [Fig. 71]; and **Origami Basket with Mickey Mouse,** be-fore 1981 [Fig. 81].) Rossbach offers his explanation of his self-deprecating, ironic use of the Mouse:

> I like Mickey Mouse. I think it's partly because it's a defensive attitude on my part. . . . They refer to the classes that you teach as Mickey Mouse classes, and everything is just dismissed as 'It's Mickey Mouse.' Somehow this is very damaging. So I put a Mickey Mouse on baskets and the most elaborate textile—I wove Mickey Mouse in double damask. (laughter) I did him on ikats. I've done a lot of Mickey Mouses.[46]

The irony of a pop image on an elegantly crafted textile makes Rossbach's vision very much in tune with Postmodernism and its use of contradictions:

> Mickey Mouse amuses me as an image. It seems ridiculous to be laboriously picking-in a Mickey Mouse in figured damask, or to work it in need-lepoint lace. In historic textiles it is so accept-able to see saints and classical figures portrayed. I think that I feel as comfortable with Mickey Mouse as those artisans felt with their saints and gods.[47]

The **Plaited Handgun,** 1975 (Fig. 75), is another example of a juxtaposition of a serious image on a fringed plaited red and white paper format which seems festive like a party favor. This startling combi-nation comments on our society and its trivialization of the serious and on the everyday quality that vio-lence has taken on in our lives. Rossbach's mature art is very much rooted in social comment. The handgun image in this work is enlarged and rendered in a sketchy way, evocative of the menacing graffiti on public walls in the Berkeley of the 60s and 70s:

> When I put an image of a handgun in my work (the first handgun was plaited in red and white

paper), I was almost certainly influenced by a painting I had seen reproduced in an art magazine. It didn't strike me at the time as a neat idea for a piece of plaiting. . . . Later, in looking through a newspaper I saw a photo of the gun used in the Kennedy assassination. It spoke to me. I xeroxed it after it had been lying around my table for awhile, and enlarged it. Then I drafted it on graph paper, and also on a diagonal graph. I like graphs as much as I like plaiting. Then I plaited a handgun image. Very much later I was walking up the stairs into the building where I was teaching [Wurster Hall]; someone had painted a handgun on the concrete tread. It was a wonderful spontaneous drawing —absolute, immediate and direct. I hoped it would remain until I got my camera—which it did. Then I enlarged my photo and Xeroxed it, and made a heat transfer of the Xerox. This image has appeared on two baskets, years apart. Naturally I think about whoever made the drawing on the stairs. I feel that when I set out to look for images to use, I am less successful than when I merely find something. The processes are entirely different.[48]

Rossbach's methods and uses of imagery look ahead to the late 1970s and 1980s fiber art where image, symbol and metaphor in textiles begin to replace purely formalist content of technique and materials.

Image is also an important element in his protest baskets and his "art about art." Both of these genres find their roots in his work from the 1960s and 1970s, and relate to developments in the fine art

92. **Treasury**, 1982
   Corrugated paper, sticks, polyethylene film tubing
   Plaited, tied
   8 3/4″ x 9 3/4″ x 9 3/4″
   Mr. and Mrs. Sanford M. Besser, Little Rock, Arkansas
   Photo: Vince Foster

world. Made over a number of years, these pieces in- corporate magazine images of El Salvador and Lebanon and express Rossbach's sadness over the destruction there. He takes a craft form, historically humble and functional like a basket, and fills it with dramatic emotion. Here, again, Rossbach is a pioneer, pushing back the boundaries of expression at a time when only a minority of artists are creating specifically polit- ical art.

Another interesting direction begun by painters of the 1960s, like Larry Rivers, and continued in ar- chitecture and design fields, is art which comments on other art. Again, it should be emphasized that Ross- bach was not necessarily looking at those sources in creating his own ''art about art,'' but was so current in his own thinking that his own work expressed what was going on elsewhere at the time. Rossbach believes that ''art builds on art. You need to know the past,'' he said. ''History is not inhibiting to me and to freshness.''[49] In his borrowing, or appropria- tion as it came to be called in the 1980s, Rossbach al- ways gives respect and credit to his sources. Of baskets and history he says:

> I don't think that an artist is ever entirely dis- sociated from historical roots. And I think that inevitably these roots influence what a contem- porary basketmaker does. The *concept* of baskets throughout history is so tied to form

93. **Sports Illustrated,** 1980
   Commercial cotton fabric, dye
   Silk screened, heat transfer printed
   140" x 42"
   Collection of the Artist

94. **Sketch for a Vestment,** 1978
   Commercial cotton fabric, dye, felt pen
   Silk screened, heat transfer printed, drawn
   46" x 27 1/2"
   Collection of the Artist

and function, and specific cultures, that all this is somehow reflected in the new baskets, no matter how free from them the contemporary basketmaker seems, or perhaps would like to be. The idea of a basket exists somehow in the artist's mind, and that idea came from some- where. Recently Lillian Elliott said something to the effect that my baskets were 'comments upon historical baskets.' I liked this. This idea keeps intriguing me—although of course I want my baskets to be more than comments —I am not a critic or historian. But I look, as often as I can at ethnic art, and quite consciously derive shapes of my baskets from ceramic forms and from glass and wooden vessels from various times and places. I don't think of them as my historical roots, except that sometimes I *do* think of them in that way. Recently I recalled that many years ago [1950] the English potter Bernard Leach was here lecturing and demon- strating. He was lamenting that American potters had no roots . . . at the same time that he him- self was adopting Japanese roots. Sometimes I feel a rather fierce awareness of my roots in the American culture—although I am sure Native Americans would feel I am presumptuous in say- ing such a thing. Increasingly, in my work I feel myself inspired by work from other cul- tures. I value the associations, and expect them to be recognized in my work. At the same time I value the differentness of my work. Baskets inspired by a foreign culture are inevitably different from baskets made within that culture. That accounts for much of the challenge and ex- citement of making baskets today.[50]

His ''art about art'' is an homage to the work from which it borrows, not an ego-inflating exercise. **Peru- vian Tunic,** 1976 (Fig. 69), shows his admiration for the formal balance and contrasts of alternating plain and patterned panels in an historical textile. Some- times historical references are humorous, as in **Early**

137

138

Cross, 1967 (Fig. 40), which was done in the very un-Coptic technique of knotted netting with pile for the figure's hair and face. The finished piece reminded him of Mrs. Cross, the neighbor across the street, its title playfully misleading. "It just delights me to think that anyone might try to find a religious significance (laughs)."[51] **Vinyl Log Cabin,** 1970 (Fig. 45), shows us a startling version of that traditional quilt pattern in heat-bonded red and white vinyl. **Toftner Square,** 1980 (Fig. 76), is a comment on 19th century Paisley shawls. **Montaña Poncho,** 1975 (Fig. 58), pays homage to textiles from the Peruvian jungle, with canvas and news paper. **Young Hercules,** 1967 (Fig. 39), looks like a Coptic textile image greatly enlarged and presented as an archaeological fragment with holes and missing parts. Again the dramatic enlargement of scale, the substitution of jute and a netting technique for the historically accurate material and technique—this total change of context—causes us to see all the references in a fresh way. Several creative concerns described by Rossbach come together in this work:

> Maybe this impulse [to change scale] was related to an interest at that time in making 'textile fragments.' When I was making textile fragments I was changing the scale, or making some other radical change—not trying to duplicate a fragment or give the effect of old age. I think

95. **Progression,** 1983
    Ash splints, rice paper, lacquer
    Diagonal plaiting
    21″ x 12″ x 12″
    Collection of the Artist

96. **Tangerine,** 1988
    Ash splints, rice paper, lacquer
    Plaited, painted
    14″ x 8 1/2″ x 9 1/2″
    Marcia Smith
    Photo: Mark Katzman

139

the 'ancient' look or the 'used' look of a few of my baskets and raffia panels derived more from looking at anthropological specimens and thinking about whether an old, worn-out look was something to work toward. I do think, now, that it related me and my work to the whole history of textiles. Also, it amused me to make my work look ancient—at the same time that other pieces of my work were looking fresh and new, shiny bright.[52]

The reasons he gives for loving to change scale show once again his originality and questioning of authority. For textile enthusiasts it could seem irreverant to make a delicate piece of lace large and strong as he does in **Bobbin Lace With Openings,** 1970 (Fig. 50). But his intent is to make the viewer reconsider a once highly valued textile seldom used today:

> I always want to change it [scale] in one direction—make things bigger, not smaller. I don't like looking at work through a diminishing glass. I love photographic enlargements. Something wonderful happens when scale is changed, upwards. Of course, something wonderful happens also when scale is changed downwards, but I'm not into that. When it is universally acknowledged that something is just right in scale, I am willing to see it in another scale, to try to understand perhaps why the original scale was 'just right,' or just to change it for the sake of being ornery. I mean, maybe revise the standards. . . . I love beautiful diagrams of textile structures. The diagrams are to me aesthetically satisfying. I love a diagram of a knot, say, that is clearly expressed to reveal the structural configuration. The next step seems to me to be to construct a knot in big scale that has the same structural clarity. This is a time [in history] of looking at little things big, and big things little. Everything vast is reduced to a minuscule formula—the workings of the universe are reduced to an equation of a few

symbols. While everything minuscule is magnified to overwhelm the universe. Why are we so intrigued by a giant enlargement of a brushstroke by Monet or Van Gogh? It is all part of a sense of wonder, of a desire to understand, or comprehend.[53]

1970s: COMING OF AGE OF FIBER ART IN THE UNITED STATES

The 1970s were vital and exciting times for the textile arts, especially in California. Many areas of investigation which Rossbach and a few others had opened up in the 50s and 60s—the rediscovery of off-loom techniques, the interest in the tangible object, the investigation of techniques and structures, the introduction of found materials, and the idea of textiles as a medium of personal expression—became in the 70s the main thrust of exploration, as many more artists began to work in fiber. Experiments were boldly stated and expansive: off-loom sculptural work predominated. Fiber even made its way into the mainstream with its appearance in *Life* and *Saturday Review* magazines in 1972, where its newness and boldness were touted.[54]

Many art ideas of the previous decade came to full flower in the 1970s. Happenings developed into performance art; attempts to reach beyond museum walls led to large site-specific works (with Christo using textiles); the interest in assemblage led to large-scale structures and the use of alternative materials like wood, cloth and plastic and mixed media; conceptual art emphasized ideas by downplaying the materiality of art; and photography and photo processes invaded all areas. Minimalism continued, but imagery made a come-back with the photo realists. Textiles became a material for the ''fine art'' world as Robert Morris, Lucas Samaras, Miriam Schapiro, Sam Gilliam and others explored this medium.

Rossbach's fiber work encompassed and anticipated many of these new directions. His use of alternative materials such as newspaper and plastic, well established by 1970, continued throughout the decade in such pieces as **Coiled Newspaper Basket,** 1974 (Fig. 60), and **Netted Newspaper,** 1975 (Fig. 63). Other fiber artists began to follow his lead, for example John Garrett and Francoise Grossen. Rossbach also made conceptual pieces like **Newspaper Knot,** 1975 (Fig. 61), an art work that is a commentary on the making rather than a finished elegant art statement. **Toftner Square,** 1980 (Fig. 76), is a sketch diagram for making a finished paisley, with schematic directions for the weave. Rossbach incorporated imagery and began to utilize photo transfer processes in his work, as in **Mad Ludwig,** 1976 (Fig. 77h), to make directly identifiable historical references.

Rossbach's was not the only influence on fiber art in the 70s. In the early part of the decade, contemporary Eastern European artists exerted the strongest influence on Americans with their powerful expressionist use of fibers. Americans could just as easily

97. **Maine Coast,** 1988
   Silk, wool, synthetic yarn
   Jacquard loom woven at the Rhode Island School of
      Design
   48″ x 26 1/2″
   Collection of the Artist

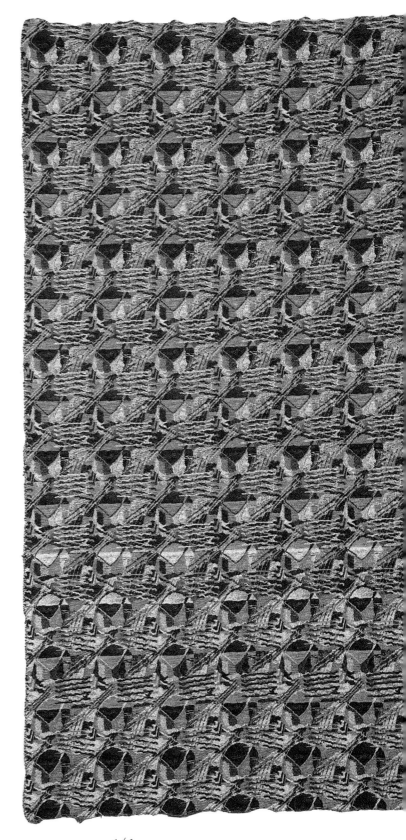

have been inspired by Dutch textile work—which, like Rossbach's, was much more classically oriented to structure, system and restraint in the tradition of Mondrian—but they were not. Perhaps Americans had had enough of minimalist geometry at that time, or maybe the emotionalism of Polish and Yugoslavian work with its heavy hanging fringes and dark gaping holes appealed more to the dramatic tenor of the times. American work in this early part of the decade often consisted of bold expressions strongly stated (or overstated), and often employed many dramatic ideas in one piece. Some American galleries were showing East European work, notably the Jacques Baruch Gallery in Chicago which opened in 1968 and from 1971 onwards showed East European fiber artists such as Magdalena Abakanowicz, whose work Rossbach saw and admired: "I was greatly impressed when I saw the work of Abakanowicz—it had emotion that seemed lacking in other contemporary fiber work."[55] Rossbach, however, clearly knew his own balance of reason and emotion. His work, while free, open and expressive was never unrestrained: the classicist's reserve was always apparent. Significant, too, is the fact that of the Europeans, it was the Dutch who included him in an important exhibition in 1976 (see below).

The 70s was the age of big exhibitions. These exhibitions, which often traveled and sometimes were accompanied by a related symposium or publication, had tremendous importance in disseminating ideas among the artists. *Objects: USA* set the standard in 1969. It was followed in 1971 by Bernard Kester's *Deliberate Entanglements,* which began at UCLA and traveled. Rossbach was not shown here or in the Lausanne *Biennales.* He was invited into *Fiberworks* in 1977 at the Cleveland Museum, but did not respond.

In 1976, however, he was included in *Structuur in Textiel* in the Netherlands, at the Stedelijk Museum in Amsterdam, an appropriate forum for his ideas on structure. The catalogue said of American fiber in general and in particular of the damask work of Rossbach's which was shown:

> The development of textile art in America shows traces of both old and new traditions; it is just as natural in that country to study ancient Peruvian weaves as the ideas of the Bauhaus, which have been passed on to today's students and artists by Anni Albers. Textiles is taught as a discipline at both universities and academies. This integration of science and art is customary in the United States. The combination is particularly clear in the work of Landis[56] and Rossbach—research visualized with great sensitivity. . . . Although the works by him included here represent only a small aspect of his oeuvre, they are so characteristic of his approach to basic structures and materials that they constitute an essential part of the exhibition despite the fact that the selection is, unfortunately, very limited.[57]

In terms of visibility and recognition for crafts-artists, the opening of the Renwick Gallery of the Smithsonian Institution in 1972 as a national showcase for crafts and design was an extremely important event. Rossbach's **Wallhanging,** 1965 (Fig. 25), is included in its permanent collection.

Books were also an important way of giving visibility to artists' work. Rossbach was included in the three important publications of the decade: *Beyond Craft,* 1973, and *The Art Fabric Mainstream*, 1981, by Constantine and Larsen, and *The Dyer's Art,* 1976-9, by Larsen (with Buhler and Solyom). The two latter

98. **Divination,** 1988
Palm bark, magnolia sticks, staples
Folded, stapled
10″ x 8″ x 6 1/2″
Collection of the Artist

books accompanied large exhibitions which toured United States museums. The trend toward large exhibitions and accompanying books continued into the 1980s: Rossbach was included in *Fiber R/Evolution*, 1986, Craft Today: *The Poetry of the Physical*, 1986, and *Interlacing: The Elemental Fabric*, 1987.

The flourishing craft movement also owed a debt to the prosperity and growth of higher education in the 60s. That expansion overflowed into the early 70s, although by 1975 teaching jobs for graduates dried up as cutbacks diminished many programs. Notably, the fiber program at University of California, Berkeley, was phased out when the College of Environmental Design reorganized its departments. Unfortunately this occurred at the time of fiber's greatest enrollment and popularity. Students who had already graduated from Rossbach's program and those who could no longer enroll at Berkeley set about creating another place where they could meet, work and exhibit. Fiberworks was established for just such a purpose in 1973 by Gyongy Laky, a former graduate student of Rossbach's. It existed as an extraordinary place until it closed its doors in 1987, when it was incorporated into a Fiber and Mixed Media Graduate Program at John F. Kennedy University in San Francisco. 1973 was the same year that students from California College of Arts and Crafts established Pacific Basin School of Textile Arts, which was more strictly textile oriented, and which remained open until 1986.

Rossbach lectured at both places, but it was Fiberworks in particular that was based on his free-ranging ideas and the mingling of traditional methods with up-to-date materials and processes. Fiberworks sought to borrow inspiration from all the arts and tapped into everything that was happening—performance art, process pieces, all kinds of media, permanent and ephemeral works. The school exemplified the passionate involvement Rossbach inspired. As Nance O'Banion, who was a graduate of the Berkeley MFA program

99. **Bison/Bison,** 1988
    Felt marker, colored pencil on paper
    Irregular rectangle, 13 3/4″ x 10 1/4″
    Mr. and Mrs. Samuel J. Rosenfeld

100. **Bison/Bison,** 1988
    Palm, commercial fabric
    Stapled, heat transfer printed
    7 1/4″ x 10″ x 6 3/4″
    Mr. and Mrs. Samuel J. Rosenfeld

101. **Buffalo Basket,** 1987
    Mexican bark paper, palm leaf, ink
    Constructed, heat transfer printed
    15″ x 16″ x 17″
    Collection of Judy and Patrick Coady
    Photos: Franko Khoury

and now teaches at California College of Arts and Crafts, and was then involved with Fiberworks said, "His own passion was really inspiring for us in terms of commitment."[58]

Rossbach, in turn, is passionate in his praise of Fiberwork's achievements:

> I identify the project with Gyongy Laky. . . . She discussed with me what she was doing, which, as I recall involved taking over a tapestry workshop with tapestry looms. When Fiberworks was in its heyday, it was an absolutely wonderful thing. I miss it, and I miss what it stood for. What an alive, forward-looking, inventive, thoughtful thing. Nothing has filled the vacancy it left—although as far as I was concerned, it had been gone long before it finally moved out. It was stimulating just thinking about Fiberworks, knowing that it existed, that it was possible. It encouraged all sorts of speculation, all sorts of possibilities. The facilities were often lousy for what it was trying to do—I remember once when I was giving a talk there, police calls kept coming over my microphone. My students could exhibit their work there when the University provided no such facilities for textiles.[59]

LATE 1970s AND 1980s: DIGESTING THE REVOLUTION

It is often the case that periods of rapid change are followed by quieter periods in which people digest, understand and learn to use the new forms. In the wake of the excitement of the preceding era, these times seem perhaps less innovative. The late 70s and 1980s have been such a time. There is much high quality work in textiles being done in the United States today, and it is built on the revolutionary experiments of Rossbach and the pioneers of the 1960s

and early 1970s. Geographically the work is more dispersed throughout the United States .than it had been when the Bay Area was clearly the center.

Rossbach's work, however, continues to be highly innovative. In step with the Postmodernism of the art world, it has gone beyond the purely formalist explorations of material and technique which marked the excitement of the earlier fiber discoveries. **Eskimo Pie,** 1987 (Fig. 89), makes an ice cream carton into a beautiful decorative object and, in the process, comments on the ordinary. **Eagle's Nest Box,** 1984 (Fig. 90), expresses admiration for nature's structures. There is still an intense interest in random and ordered structures and the intricate and skilled uses of many historic techniques in his work (and generally in the fiber world). In retrospect one can see that his studies of structure were rarely just formalist after the 1950s, even in an Op Art piece like **Equivocal Cube,** 1969 (Fig. 49), because the technique and its associations are partly the subject of the piece. Either he comments on the meaning of ordinary objects, on the marvel of textile methods, or on intricacy itself, as exemplified by **Damask Mickey Mouse,** 1976 (Fig. 71); the **Brocaded Silks,** 1976 (Fig. 77), with their tiny heat transfer images; **Layered Mesh,** 1970 (Fig. 41); and **Bobbin Lace with Openings,** 1970 (Fig. 50).

The 1980s have seen a renewed interest in image, and in symbol, allegory and metaphor. Narrative devices appear in both sculpture and in two dimensional art forms. The new imagery is especially related to semiotics, a major intellectual and artistic preoccupation of the 1980s. His images often interact with titles, sometimes are visual puns or mixed references, like **Early Cross,** 1964 (Fig. 40), **Sketch for a Vestment,** 1978 (Fig. 94) or **Eskimo Pie,** 1987 (Fig. 89), and deal with how we see or do not see—in other words, how signs and referents do or do not communicate, and how humorous that process often is. His concerns are similar to those of semiotics:

102. **Log,** 1988
Eucalyptus bark
Folded, stapled
13″ x 5 1/2″ x 5 1/2″
Collection of Judy and Patrick Coady
Photo: Franko Khoury

It seems so interesting to me how textile images linger in our culture from one generation to the next. I love seeing the paisley motif everywhere. And, I am amused watching television, to see the Chinese dignitaries meeting George Schultz, or James Baker, or whoever, in a room in China with French Baroque upholstery and Baroque wallpaper. And so on. The decorative arts keep lingering with all their messages and their abilities to establish feelings, environments, etc. At the same time, it is very funny.[60]

Communication is very important to Rossbach's work, which does not strive to be deliberately unreadable like much of abstract art.[61] He expresses frustration when that communication does not occur:

Very many of my textiles use imagery from eighteenth century brocaded silks, which I am fond of, and which I studied for a number of years. Surprisingly the imagery is esoteric today, and seldom recognized—which is unsatisfactory to me because I consider recognition of the images, and associations with them, to be of utmost importance if the viewer is to react fully.[62]

Rossbach also communicates directly in his writing:

I am surprised to realize how closely related were my writing, my creative work, and my teaching. . . . During all my years in Berkeley I was involved in writing. Most of it was never published, partly because I never, did anything about trying to get it published. My writing was like much of my creative activity in textiles — something that seemed satisfying and worthwhile in itself — it didn't need to go any further. So that much of my writing was never read by anyone, just as much of my textile work was never exhibited. This was not entirely satisfactory to me. I always found pleasure in having my work exhibited and my writing published.[63]

Of the creative aspect of writing he says:

I wanted to write with a freedom that I never

146

achieved except perhaps in the little 'artist books' that I made, one after another. (See **The Weaver's Secret Book,** 1977 [Fig. 74].) I felt that in them I could express my nuttiness, and some of the thoughts that were in my mind. I believe (probably no one would agree) that my writing on textiles is a sort of personal expression. My books have been as satisfying to me as my textile work. The writing never comes easy—I wish it would flow—but I agonize over it, change, and change, and change. . . . You would think that after all this writing I would be better at it.[64]

> A warp must always be perceived as an organic whole. It must also be perceived as a system.
> A warp requires proper resolution.
> Questions and answers:
> Q. Which historical textiles have high resolution?
> A. The great ones.

(from **The Weaver's Secret Book,** 1977 [Fig. 74])[65]

Many artists of the 1980s discovered that objects communicate a power and presence in their tangibility, a kind of magical presence associated with tribal cultures' use and ritual.[66] Rossbach's baskets speak of remnants or artifacts of some strange culture as well as of our own. Their small hand-held utilitarian forms make them disturbingly personal: that is what makes them so powerful. **Dark Indian,** 1987 (Fig. 3), and **Homage to Richard Wagner,** 1985 (Fig. 85), have a slightly sinister quality about them: it is those life-scale photographs of faces or eyes, half hidden and close to us.

Rossbach's interest in recognizable imagery led to photography and other image-duplicating processes like Xerox and heat transfers. The use of photography also grew in part out of his extensive travels, historical research of textiles, and understanding of historical context. The camera accompanies the Rossbachs on most of their travels, and the folk art they collect on the trips accompanies them home. This folk art fills the Rossbach home with colorful, often humorous objects. He draws inspiration from this collection and even taught a course in folk art at Berkeley in the early 1960s. Folk art speaks to the childlike, naive, fresh quality in him which is so apparent in his work. Of this interest he said with this typical ingredient of paradox: "I love folk art. I imagine I could be very satisfied just being a folk artist. But then other times I don't think I could be that at all. At the same time I want to be sophisticated."[67] That childlike freshness is one of the most influential elements of Rossbach's character. Because of it, he embraces change and can love things which are evanescent. He laments that in our society there is such a concentration on the object and the product:

> Someone has to speak out for no product . . . the joy in doing . . . the satisfaction of just looking at something and it's gone. . . . It's kind of out of our time to value anything that has no value. It's so important that somebody take a stand about this . . . [something] that is fresh and spontaneous that somebody did in two minutes and found tremendous joy in doing.[68]

Rossbach will certainly be remembered for that spontaneity. He will be remembered for making the old, long forgotten techniques of textiles live again for us and for teaching us new ways to think about them as avenues of artistic expression. He will be remembered for reminding us that textiles are the tangible markers of a person's relationship to society. He showed us that any material can be beautiful, and that the value of an art object is not only in its material substance but also in the idea that is embodied in it and shared with the viewer.

NOTES

Ed Rossbach

[1] Charles Edmund Rossbach: Artist, Mentor, Professor, Writer. Interview with Harriet Nathan, Copy 14, Fiber Arts Oral History Series, Regional Oral History Office, The Bancroft Library, University of California, Berkeley. (Hereafter cited in text as OH followed by page number of reference.)

[2] Ed Rossbach n.d.d.

[3] Ed Rossbach n.d.i.

[4] Ed Rossbach 1982c.

[5] Ed Rossbach n.d.i.

[6] Ed Rossbach n.d.i.

[7] Ed Rossbach n.d.i.

[8] Ed Rossbach n.d.i.

[9] Ed Rossbach n.d.i.

[10] Ed Rossbach 1973a, 8.

[11] Ed Rossbach n.d.i.

[12] Ed Rossbach 1984b, 9.

[13] Ed Rossbach 1984b, 10.

[14] Ed Rossbach n.d.i.

[15] See Larsen, Buhler, and Solyom 1977; Constantine and Larsen 1973 and 1981; Larsen and Freudenheim 1987 for major publications.

[16] See Janeiro 1988; Westphal 1976.

[17] Ed Rossbach n.d.k.

[18] Ed Rossbach 1982c, 10.

[19] Ed Rossbach n.d.i.

[20] Ed Rossbach n.d.i.

[21] Ed Rossbach n.d.i.

[22] Ed Rossbach n.d.i.

[23] Ed Rossbach n.d.i.

[24] Ed Rossbach n.d.i.

[25] Ed Rossbach n.d.i.

[26] Ed Rossbach n.d.i.

[27] Ed Rossbach n.d.i.

[28] Ed Rossbach n.d.i.

[29] Ed Rossbach n.d.i.

[30] Ed Rossbach n.d.i.

[31] Rossbach has at least two manuscripts which remain unpublished as of yet, including one book on 18th century French Brocades and another on basketry.

[32] Ed Rossbach 1973a, 16.

[33] West 1982, 31.

[34] West 1982, 33.

Textile Explorations

[1] This and all other uncredited information in this essay is derived from Ed Rossbach n.d.f and n.d.h.

[2] Ed Rossbach 1982b, 17. Strengell in Albers et al. 1948, 34.

[3] The flossa technique has the supplementary weft pile formed by wrapping the weft over a rod. The loops thus formed are usually cut before the rod is removed, although sometimes a contrasting area of uncut loops is retained as part of the design. The structure formed by this method is the same as the so-called "Ghiordes knot" so common in Oriental rugs. The same structure also is characteristic of rya, in which the pile is formed using pre-cut lengths of supplementary weft. In practice, flossa also has a shorter denser pile than rya. See Cyrus 1956, 210-220.

[4] Illustrated in Thurman 1983, 205, Fig. 167 (black and white).

[5] Both are illustrated in Miller 1948, 22-23.

[6] Harrison 1948.

[7] O'Neale 1932, 1945. The Peruvian publications began with O'Neale and Kroeber 1930.

[8] O'Neale 1946, O'Neale and Clark 1948.

[9] Information on Gayton from Boyer 1978. Ruth Boyer, who also had a Ph.D. in anthropology and a major interest in folklore, was Gayton's successor from 1965-71. She unfortunately did not receive tenure since the department was by then being phased out.

[10] Ed Rossbach n.d.e, 88-89.

[11] Rossbach 1948, 21.

[12] His opinions on the art vs. craft debate are expressed in his 1981 article. His favorite definition of art is "if you say it's art, it's art."

[13] Rossbach 1971, 13.

[14] Also illustrated in Thurman 1983, Pl. 49 (color). Another upholstery fabric, from 1952, is illustrated in Fig. 168. This piece has a check pattern which correlates with a grid of a plain-weave derived float weave. Both the color and texture changes are subtle.

[15] Also illustrated in Larsen, Adams and Riley 1961, 33, no. 11; Constantine and Larsen (1973, 218) have some perceptive comments on this piece. It was submitted to a juried textile exhibition at the University of Washington in Seattle in 1951 along with a grass mat. Both works won prizes. However, since there was in fact no money for these prizes the works were auctioned off. Larsen bought the casement, later giving it to the Brooklyn Museum. The mat was never photographed and is now lost.

[16] Also illustrated in Thurman 1983, 207, Pl. 48 (color).

[17] Atwater 1928 contains a chapter on this construction (Part II, Chapter 14; 1951, Chapter 13). For an insightful assessment of Atwater's role in twentieth century handweaving, see Ed Rossbach 1983.

[18] Ed Rossbach 1976a, 29-30.

[19] Ed Rossbach 1976a, 34. An example of a Liebes blind can be found in Znamierowski 1970, 18. This piece dates from 1952.

[20] Ed Rossbach 1955a, 26.

[21] Ed Rossbach 1954 and 1955b. The uncredited examples illustrated are by Rossbach. The screen in Part I (1954), Fig. 8 has a flax warp and raffia weft. The warp has random gauze crosses causing openings between the wefts. Another screen in Part II (1955b), Fig. 2 is in plain weave with a silk warp, and cellophane, reed, and raffia wefts.

[22] Also illustrated in Ed Rossbach 1955b, 18, Fig. 3. The reeds are here described as Japanese, though Rossbach now recollects them as being African. In Ed Rossbach n.d.j, he describes them as "very hard, and beautiful in brownish color."

[23] Constantine and Larsen 1973, 219.

[24] The tule is a rush of the sedge family, Scirpus spp., that grows abundantly in wet lands or water.

[25] Ed Rossbach n.d.i.

[26] See for example Roth 1918, 27-41 and Loir 1935.

[27] Ed Rossbach n.d.e, 80.

[28] Ed Rossbach n.d.d. See also Ed Rossbach 1976a, 47-48.

[29] **Blue Ikat** (1957, in the collection of the Metropolitan Museum of Art), illustrated in Brite 1986, 41 (color), is another particularly beautiful example.

[38] Also illustrated in Nagle 1960, no. 108. I asked Rossbach if he minded the idea of his ikats being draped and he said no. Curtain-like vertical folds would do interesting things to the ikat designs.

[31] Ed Rossbach n.d.d.

[32] Examples are illustrated in Nagle 1960, nos. 109-111.

[33] Rossbach (n.d.h.) said he used yarns leftover from another ikat for this piece, alternated with non-ikatted warps in order to obtain a full loom width. However, this does not mean that the effect obtained was not fully intentional.

[34] This piece was shown in the Milan *Triennale* in 1964.

[35] Ed Rossbach n.d.i.

[36] An example with stencilled and painted warps is illustrated in Held 1973, 286, Pl. 33.

[37] Rossbach's original fabric was included in the traveling exhibition that Larsen organized in 1961, *Fabrics International*, and is illustrated in color on the cover of the catalogue as well as the cover of the Sept./Oct. 1961 issue of *Craft Horizons*. This was of course how the fabric came to Larsen's attention. Rossbach had not titled his piece. The name **Bamako** derives from the fact that Larsen gave African names to his collection that year (1962-63). The original fabric is also illustrated in Thurman 1983, 206, Pl. 47 (where it is erroneously described as Larsen's adaptation). Rossbach (n.d.j) no longer remembers clearly whether he used temporary wefts in this piece or simply held areas of warp in position with sticks; he thinks probably the latter.

[38] Also illustrated in Larsen, Buhler and Solyom 1977, 231 (detail).

[39] Also illustrated in Larsen, Buhler and Solyom 1977, 215.

[40] Also illustrated in Held 1978, 168, Fig. 291 (detail). The double cloth mentioned in the next sentence is illustrated in Campbell 1960, 26 center.

[41] An example of his tie dye is illustrated in Larsen 1978, 30.

[42] The Mimbres pottery style flourished in southwestern New Mexico between about 1000 and 1100 A.D. and had black geometric or animal designs on a white ground. A hole was frequently deliberately drilled in the bottom of Mimbres bowls prior to burial with the dead. Rossbach's piece is also illustrated in Thurman 1983, 203, Pl. 46 (color).

[43] Ed Rossbach 1978, 29.

[44] From an exhibit catalogue, dated January 1981. **Toftner Square** is also illustrated.

[45] Noted in Ed Rossbach 1976a, 37.

[46] See Goodall 1966, 32. Ironically enough, only a detail is

shown, as if the piece were in fact yardage!

[47] Ed Rossbach 1950, 41.

[48] An interesting unfinished piece is illustrated in Harcourt 1962, Pl. 5.

[49] Also illustrated in Larsen, Kaufmann and Forberg 1964, 31; Constantine and Larsen 1973, 222, though this photograph is overexposed. The title that appears in the Constantine and Larsen book, **Tapestry,** was not given to the piece by Rossbach and indeed he objects to it since the piece is not really tapestry weave.

[50] Ed Rossbach n.d.g. The Mondrian quote used here is so basic to his philosophy that it appears in Janson 1962, 525. I am grateful to Rebecca Stevens for bringing this quotation to my attention.

[51] This structure is illustrated in Emery 1966, 183, Fig. 286.

[52] West 1982, 31. It was also clear from a lecture he gave at The Textile Museum in 1981.

[53] Illustrated in Constantine and Larsen 1969, no. 23; 1973, 225 top (color detail); Held 1973, 88, Fig. 143. Related pieces include **Detroit** (1968), also in Constantine and Larsen 1969, no. 22; **Hanging Wall** (1969), illustrated in Nordness 1970, 324-5; a work made of plastic tubing stuffed with foam (1968) shown in the process of being created in Constantine and Larsen 1973, 225 bottom.

[54] Ed Rossbach, n.d.d.

[55] Quoted in Slivka 1976, no. 45.

[56] Ed Rossbach n.d.d.

[57] Ed Rossbach 1973a, 50; 1986, 62. He has just been discussing temporary baskets preserved in museum collections, but the statement is as valid for his own works in perishable materials.

[58] Ed Rossbach n.d.e, 131 and n.d.f. Rossbach said he had seen a Hicks piece in the design section at the Museum of Modern Art in New York. Some examples are illustrated in Kaufman 1968, 10 and color plate III; Constantine and Larsen 1969, Pl. 8.

[59] Illustrated in West 1982, 32 bottom.

[60] Illustrated in Held 1978, 140, Fig. 233.

[61] **World Egg** is also illustrated in Harvey 1972, Fig. 3-7. **Macrame** is also illustrated in Harvey 1972, Pl. C-8 (color); Constantine and Larsen 1973, 223; Press 1988, no. 28.

[62] **Christmas Basket** is also illustrated in Story 1972. **Ceremonial Plate with Face** is also illustrated in Harvey 1972, Pl. C-7 (color). A related piece, **Ceremonial Plate with Apocalyptic Face** (1965), is illustrated in Constantine and

[63] Larsen 1973, 221 bottom.

[63] Ed Rossbach n.d.i. This piece belongs to The Council House, The International Conference Center of S.C. Johnson & Son, Inc., Racine, Wisconsin. Illustrated in Moseley 1966; Nordness 1970, 325 right; 1980, 184 (color).

[64] Also illustrated in Constantine and Larsen 1969, no. 21; 1973, 224 (color).

[65] Illustrated in Anonymous 1966, 39; Stevens 1981, 17; West 1982, 33 top.

[66] Ed Rossbach 1973a, 67, Fig. 80, and 91, Fig. 115.

[67] Ed Rossbach 1984a, 70.

[68] A looped piece of similar texture but with a design of rectangles more reminiscent of Peruvian textiles is illustrated in Chamberlain and Crockett 1974, 90 top (color).

[69] Illustrated in Constantine and Larsen 1981, 77 (detail); Press 1988, no. 29 (full view). The Peruvian technique is shown in Harcourt 1962, 130, Fig. 94, and Pls. 40-44.

[70] See for instance, Harcourt 1962, 110 and 112, Fig. 81. However, when I asked Rossbach (n.d.f) whether he had used Harcourt to learn this technique, he said no. This piece was exhibited in San Diego (Parks 1971).

[71] Also illustrated in Ed Rossbach 1976a, 6 and 40, Fig. 24.

[72] Also illustrated in Hall 1977, 99, Pl. 107 (color); Press 1988, no. 33. Rossbach remade this piece for the *Knots and Nets* exhibition.

[73] Quoted in Constantine and Larsen 1973, 227 bottom in a caption for an illustration of this piece. Another example of Rossbach's needle lace, with an abstract design, is illustrated on the same page, top.

[74] **Small White Lace** illustrated in D. Smith 1970, 55; Constantine and Larsen 1973, 226; Bath 1974, 211. **White and Yellow Lace** is illustrated in Held 1978, 23, Fig. 34. **Points de Genes I**, a large piece with an interlaced structure, is illustrated in K. Rossbach 1970, 17 (detail).

[75] I am indebted to verbal description and close-up photos from Sara Green to clarify this construction.

[76] Also illustrated in West 1982, 33 bottom (detail).

[77] The term plaiting is used by Rossbach and others to refer to non-loom interlacing, though it is not used in this way by Emery. Emery's definition does not appear to be either useful or justified (see Rowe 1985). Having installed a version of Jack Lenor Larsen's Interlacing exhibition, it appears most useful to me to use the term for a technique as opposed to a structure. Since other names are available for other non-loom interlacing techniques such as braiding, sprang, and bobbin

lace, it might be most useful to use the term plaiting for the technique of interlacing without any tools and without fixing the elements at one or both ends first.

[78] Ed Rossbach 1973b, 28.

[79] Other examples not shown here include: **Plaited Square** (1975), illustrated in Constantine and Larsen 1981, 79 bottom, made of rumpled strips of brown wrapping paper; and a mat made of plastic palm leaves illustrated in Ed Rossbach 1976b, 25 left.

[80] Ed Rossbach n.d.i.

[81] Three related pieces are illustrated in Ed Rossbach 1976b, 23, 24 right, 25 right.

[82] Illustrated in Constantine and Larsen 1981, 80. Unfortunately, this piece is no longer extant. A smaller related piece is shown in Ed Rossbach 1976b, 24 top left.

[83] Rossbach's piece is also illustrated in Hall 1977, 98, Pl. 106 (detail); Held 1978, 241, Fig. 442; Constantine and Larsen 1981, 60-61.

[84] Illustrated in Moore 1968; Constantine and Larsen 1973, 221 left; Chamberlain and Crockett 1974, 90 bottom (color).

[85] Ed Rossbach n.d.i (also n.d.f). These two baskets and one other were exhibited at Museum West in 1965 and at the Museum of Contemporary Crafts in 1968. The third basket was made in lace techniques of jute cord. ''I made components which I then assembled. Of course it wouldn't stand up, and I had to gesso it liberally to stiffen it. I recalled the time when I was a child, when women used to crochet nut cups for children's parties. These were then stiffened with sugar.'' (Ed Rossbach n.d.i).

[86] Rossbach selected some Textile Museum objects for an exhibition to be held concurrently with the retrospective of his work. The idea was to select pieces that had a particular aesthetic appeal for him. Since the Museum has a very strong archaeological textile collection, including both Peruvian and Coptic textiles, which interest him very much, he looked at many such pieces in the course of making his selection. In a number of instances, he thought the broken and stained areas added to the aesthetic appeal of the piece.

[87] Examples of the Ischia baskets are illustrated in Ed Rossbach 1973a, 56, Fig. 62 and 160, Fig. 195. Rossbach's piece is also illustrated in Slivka 1968, 171, Pl. 285; Nordness 1970, 326.

[88] Illustrated in Rossbach 1976a, 112, Fig. 126. Exhibited at the Museum of Contemporary Crafts in 1968.

[89] Ed Rossbach n.d.i.

[90] Such a diagram occurs in *American Fabrics* 1965, 80 left.

[91] Ed Rossbach 1973a, 162-165.

[92] Illustrated in K. Rossbach 1970, 17; Pulleyn 1986, 16 top right.

[93] Illustrated in Brookfield Craft Center 1974; Pulleyn 1986, 16 lower right. Unfortunately, this piece was never returned from its most recent exhibition.

[94] The appeal of this idea is stated repeatedly in Ed Rossbach 1973a. See also Malarcher 1984, 37; this article also contains an illustration of a Rossbach basket (34 bottom).

[95] K. Rossbach 1970, 17.

[96] Ed Rossbach 1973b, 30.

[97] Katherine Rossbach has written eloquently on her husband's baskets (1970). The same group is illustrated in Constantine and Larsen 1973, 75.

[98] Ed Rossbach 1973b, 30.

[99] P. Smith 1972 (unpaginated); Constantine and Larsen 1973, 228-229; Harvey 1974, 73, Figs. 6-3, 6-4.

[100] The Iroquois basket is illustrated in Ed Rossbach 1973a, 138, Fig. 168.

[101] Also illustrated Glashausser and Westfall 1976, 138 bottom.

[102] A few plaited baskets from India with odd shapes are illustrated in Ed Rossbach 1973a, 133, Figs. 159-60, and 168, Fig. 205. **Butterfly Basket** is also illustrated in Pulleyn 1986, 19, upper left (color). Another sculptural piece, **Burning Log**, is illustrated in Glashausser and Westfall 1976, 138 top.

[103] Ed Rossbach n.d.j. He also used the Iranian rabbit on some of his silks (Hagberg 1972).

[104] A related piece is illustrated in Pulleyn 1986, 19 top right.

[105] A related basket is in Slivka 1976, no. 45. Another is illustrated in Ed Rossbach 1976a, 112, Fig. 125; the same or a similar piece is in Held 1978, 90, Fig. 138.

[106] The one shown here is also illustrated in J. Brandford 1976, 17, no. C-25; also exhibited in Lausanne. A very similar basket which appears to have one extra coil is shown in Pulleyn 1986, 16 lower left. Another similar basket (1974) that has two instead of four vertical ribs and a horizontal rib on the second coil from the top is illustrated in Ed Rossbach 1976a, 110, Fig. 123; Constantine and Larsen 1981, 149 bottom (color); West 1982, 32 top.

[107] This piece has also been illustrated in Ed Rossbach 1976b, 24 bottom; Pulleyn 1986, 19 lower left (color).

[108] Ed Rossbach 1973a, 134, Fig. 162.

[109] See also **Two Forms** 1983, illustrated in Larsen and Freudenheim 1987, 256, Pl. 282. The larger form has 2/2 interlacing on the bottom and 1/1 interlacing at the top, the change not

precisely correlating with the bands of applied paper.

[110] A closely related piece, **Red Hunk** (1985), is illustrated in Smith and Smith 1986, Pl. 194.

[111] A related piece is illustrated in Pulleyn 1986, 19, lower right.

[112] Also illustrated in Pulleyn 1986, 18 (color).

[113] Also illustrated in Constantine and Larsen 1981, 156.

[114] Oka 1967.

[115] A very similar **Origami Basket**, dated 1981, is illustrated in Pulleyn 1986, 17.

[116] Ed Rossbach n.d.i. Also illustrated in Ed Rossbach 1984c, 60.

[117] Ed Rossbach 1973a, Pl. 14.

[118] Ed Rossbach n.d.i. He describes the making of this piece in Ed Rossbach 1984c, 60, 61 (color photo). Another protest basket is illustrated in Rowley 1984, 67.

[119] Another example of such a basket is **Patti LaBelle**, 1986, illustrated in Pulleyn 1986, 11. This piece is made of newspaper and has an asymmetrical shape. Another piece, **Carton Basket** (1987) is illustrated in Mayer 1988, 125. Yet another is in Hammel 1988, 168 upper left; it uses paper that has a photocopy of triaxial plaiting on it.

[120] See Rowley 1984, 67.

[121] Ed Rossbach n.d.j.

[122] An example, **Mad Ludwig II** (1979), is illustrated in Constantine and Larsen 1981, 100 bottom.

[123] Ed Rossbach n.d.d.

[124] Crommelin 1976, unpaginated.

[125] Also illustrated in Constantine and Larsen 1981, 141 bottom.

[126] See **Colored Square**, illustrated in Constantine and Larsen 1981, 166 (detail). Some of these pieces were included in the Museum of Modern Art's *Wall Hangings: The New Classicism*, in 1977 (Marein 1977).

[127] Marcoux 1982 (unpaginated). See also Ed Rossbach 1982a.

[128] Kaufmann 1950, 16. Cited in Ed Rossbach 1973a, 191.

Ed Rossbach: Educator

[1] Ed Rossbach n.d.e, 25-26.

[2] Ed Rossbach n.d.i.

[3] Constantine and Larsen 1973, 220.

[4] Ed Rossbach n.d.e.

[5] Ed Rossbach n.d.e, 86.

[6] Hickman n.d.

[7] Webb n.d.

[8] Hickman n.d.

[9] Curtis 1982, 9.

[10] Peterson n.d.

[11] Laky n.d.

[12] McQueen n.d.

[13] Park 1979, 25.

[14] McQueen n.d.

[15] Ed Rossbach n.d.i.

Rossbach in Context

[1] Hall 1977, 98.

[2] Regarding the late 1960s as a beginning of interest in folk art, see for example Blaesdel 1968.

[3] Ed Rossbach n.d.i.

[4] Ed Rossbach n.d.i.

[5] Rose 1975, 212.

[6] Ed Rossbach n.d.i.

[7] Jacob 1985, 53.

[8] In ca. 1983, Rossbach made a special visit to Gunta Stolzl in Switzerland. She had been the head of the Bauhaus weaving workshop beginning in 1926.

[9] Naylor 1968, 34.

[10] Brandford 1952. As quoted in Naylor 1968, 50.

[11] Ed Rossbach 1948, 21.

[12] Ed Rossbach n.d.c.

[13] Ed Rossbach n.d.i.

[14] Ed Rossbach n.d.b.

[15] Ed Rossbach n.d.i.

[16] Ed Rossbach n.d.i.

[17] Ed Rossbach n.d.b.

[18] Waller 1977, 10.

[19] Ed Rossbach n.d.e, 88-89.

[20] Ed Rossbach n.d.b. Rossbach is concerned to set the record straight that Lea Miller was the first to do these gauzes and use plastic. Mention also made in Ed Rossbach n.d.d.

[21] Albright 1985.

[22] Ed Rossbach n.d.c.

[23] Steinberg 1972. In this seminal essay, Steinberg explains, especially on pages 84-91, what Rauschenberg's bringing painting off the wall in his combines meant to art. Rossbach's move into three dimensional objects and found materials occurred in the 1960s and later, and he was not involved, as was Rauschenberg, in changing the nature of painting. Rossbach's experiments were more involved in combining weaving, painting and sculptural 3-D elements into object-like forms. But his breaking down of divisions between painting and sculpture or object seem to have been very much influenced by Rauschenberg's revolution. As Steinberg explains, those changes in the nature of the picture plane in painting were more far reaching: "Yet this internal change is no more than a symptom of changes which go far beyond questions of picture planes, or of painting as such. It is part of a shakeup which contaminates all purified categories. The deepening inroads of art into non-art continue to alienate the connoisseur as art defects and departs into strange territories leaving the old stand-by criteria to rule an eroding plain." (91)

[24] Ed Rossbach n.d.i.

[25] These late 1960s minimalist artists who were interested in systems have been called Systemic Artists by Lawrence Alloway. See Alloway 1975, 76-91; also in Guggenheim Museum, 1966, Systemic Painting, catalog of exhibition, 11-20.

[26] Ed Rossbach n.d.b.

[27] Ed Rossbach n.d.d.

[28] Ed Rossbach 1980, 46-47.

[29] Larsen, Kaufmann and Forberg 1964, 28.

[30] Constantine and Larsen 1973, 220.

[31] For Robert Rauschenberg's work see Alloway 1976, 3-25. For the Duchamp revival in the late 1950s and early 1960s see Tomkins 1978, 63-64, where, among other things, the large retrospective show of 1963 at the Pasadena Museum is mentioned.

[32] Centre International de la Tapisserie 1967, xxxii.

[33] Ed Rossbach n.d.h.

[34] Mare n.d.

[35] Constantine and Larsen 1969; Nordness 1970.

[36] Zeisler n.d.

[37] Elliott 1986, 9-13. She is probably referring to pieces by Kai Chan, Pat Hickman/Lillian Elliott, Katuhiro Fujimura, and Suellen Glashausser.

[38] Ed Rossbach n.d.b.

[39] Clark 1979, 310. He cites Lee Nordness as source.

[40] Ed Rossbach n.d.c.

[41] Ed Rossbach n.d.i and Ed Rossbach n.d.d.

[42] Selz 1985, 325-26.

[43] Story 1972.

[44] Selz 1985, 326.

[45] Ed Rossbach 1976b, 80.

[46] Ed Rossbach n.d.e, 91.

[47] Ed Rossbach n.d.i.

[48] Ed Rossbach n.d.i.

[49] Ed Rossbach n.d.b.

[50] Ed Rossbach n.d.i.

[51] Ed Rossbach n.d.e, 91.

[52] Ed Rossbach n.d.i.

[53] Ed Rossbach n.d.i.

[54] Life 1972; Shorr 1972.

[55] Ed Rossbach n.d.i.

[56] Richard Landis, an American born in 1931, lived in Arizona at the time of this exhibition.

[57] Crommelin 1976.

[58] Curtis 1982, 10.

[59] Ed Rossbach n.d.i.

[60] Ed Rossbach n.d.i.

[61] Kuspit 1989.

[62] Ed Rossbach n.d.i.

[63] Ed Rossbach n.d.i.

[64] Ed Rossbach n.d.i.

[65] Ed Rossbach n.d.a.

[66] For a discussion of this see White 1986.

[67] Ed Rossbach n.d.c.

[68] Ed Rossbach n.d.d.

APPENDIX

ED ROSSBACH

HONORS

1975   Appointed Fellow of the Collegium of Craftsmen of the American Crafts Council, June 10, 1975

1985   Selected as Living Treasure of California by Creative Arts League, Sacramento, California

SELECTED ONE PERSON EXHIBITIONS

1968   *Constructed and Printed Textiles*, University Art Collection, Arizona State University, Tempe, Arizona

1970   *Plastic Constructions*, Lee Nordness Galleries, New York, New York

1972   *New Work*, Anneberg Gallery, San Francisco, California

1976   *Structural Disintegration*, Fiberworks Gallery, Berkeley, California

1981   *Baskets*, Fiberworks Gallery, Berkeley, California

1986   *One Man Exhibition*, Berkeley Community Center, Berkeley, California

SELECTED TWO PERSON EXHIBITIONS

1952   *Textiles*, University of Florida, Gainsville, Florida

1952   *Textiles*, Oakland Art Museum, Oakland, California

1966   *Textiles: Ed Rossbach and Katherine Westphal*, Museum West, San Francisco

1968   *Textiles: Katherine Westphal/ Ed Rossbach*, Museum of Contemporary Crafts, New York, New York

1970   *Textiles* (with Katherine Westphal), San Diego Jewish Community Center, San Diego, California

1972   *Recent Textiles* (with Katherine Westphal), Cornell College, University of California, Santa Cruz, California

1974   Untitled exhibiton (with Katherine Westphal), Clay and Fiber Gallery, Taos, New Mexico

1983   *Baskets*, University Art Collection, Arizona State University, Tempe, Arizona

1984   *New Baskets* (with Lillian Elliott), Berkeley Community Center, Berkeley, California

SELECTED GROUP EXHIBITIONS AND AWARDS

1946   *International Textile Exhibition*, Women's College, University of North Carolina, Greensboro, North Carolina (Second Prize)

1947   *Exhibition of Michigan Artist-Craftsmen*, Detroit Artists Market, The Detroit Institute of Arts, Detroit, Michigan

1947   *International Textile Exhibition*, Women's College, University of North Carolina, Greensboro, North Carolina (Two First Prizes)

1950   *Second Annual Decorative Arts Exhibition*, San Francisco Museum of Art, San Francisco, California (Two Honorable Mentions)

1951   *First International Textile Exhibition*, Henry Art Gallery, University of Washington, Seattle, Washington (First Prize and Second Prize)

1952   *International Textile Exhibition*, Women's College, University of North Carolina, Greensboro, North Carolina (First Prize and Two Honorable Mentions)

1952   *California State Fair Open Air Show*, State Fairground, Sacramento, California (First Prize)

1954   *12th International Textile Exhibition*, Women's College, University of North Carolina, Greensboro, North Carolina (Second Prize)

1954   *Third Annual Exhibition*, Richmond Art Center, Richmond, California

1955   *United Nations Exhibition*, San Francisco Museum of Art, San Francisco, California

1956   *Craftsmanship in the Changing World*, Museum of Contemporary Crafts, New York, New York

1957 *6th Annual Decorative Arts Competition*, Civic Center, Richmond, California (First Prize)

1958 *Design for Contemporary Interiors*, Museum of Contemporary Crafts, New York, New York

1958 Untitled exhibition, U.S. Pavilion, Brussels World Fair, Brussels, Belgium

1960 *Visual Communication in the Crafts*, Museum of Contemporary Crafts, New York, New York

1960 *American Weaving*, The Walker Art Center, Minneapolis, Minnesota

1960 *Designer-Craftsmen USA 1960*, Museum of Contemporary Crafts, New York, New York

1961 *Director's Choice*, Philadelphia College of Art Gallery, Philadelphia, Pennsylvania

1964 *Design for Production*, Museum of Contemporary Crafts, New York, New York

1964 *13th Triennale di Milano*, Palazzo dell'Atre al Parco, Milan, Italy

1966 *Craftsmen USA '66*, Museum of Contemporary Crafts, New York, New York

1966 *Threads of History*, American Foundation of the Arts, New York, New York

1967 *Acquisitions*, Museum of Contemporary Crafts, New York, New York

1967 *Invitational Craft Show 1967*, Ball State University, Muncie, Indiana

1968 *Eight Artist-Craftsmen*, Western Washington State College, Spokane, Washington

1968 *California Design X*, Pasadena Art Museum, Pasadena, California

1968 *Invitational Crafts Show/1968*, St. Cloud State College, St. Cloud, Minnesota

1968 *University Art Collection*, University Art Collection Gallery, Arizona State University, Tempe, Arizona

1969 *Objects: USA*, National Collection of Fine Arts, Smithsonian Institution, Washington, DC

1969 *Fibre Structures*, University of Wisconsin, Milwaukee, Wisconsin

1969 *Excellence of the Object*, Museum of Contemporary Crafts, New York, New York

1969 *Wall Hangings*, The Museum of Modern Art, New York, New York

1969 *Fibers / Fabrics*, John Michael Kohler Arts Center, Sheboygan, Wisconsin

1969 *Survey*, Fine Arts Gallery, San Diego,. California

1970 *The Magic of Fibers*, Grand Rapids Art Museum, Grand Rapids, Michigan

1970 *Second National Craft Invitational*, Northern Illinios University, De Kalb, Illinois

1972 *Sculpture in Fiber*, Museum of Contemporary Crafts, New York, New York

1972 *Fiber by American Artists*, Ball State University, Muncie, Indiana

1973 *Comment on Contemporary Crafts*, Fine Arts Gallery, University of Wisconsin, Milwaukee, Wisconsin

1974 *Painted and Dyed*, Santa Rosa State College, Santa Rosa, California

1974 *Con-Tex-Ture*, Fort Wayne Public Library, Designer / Craftsmen Guild, Fort Wayne, Indiana

1974 *Fiber Forms . . . Past and Present*, Brookfield Craft Center, Brookfield, Connecticut

1976 *Fiber Art*, University of Illinois, Urbana, Illinois

1976 *Bag Show*, Community Center, Walnut Creek, California

1976 *The Art of Fiber*, Chevron Gallery, San Francisco, California

1976 *The North American Basket 1790-1976*, The Craft Center, Worcester, Massachusetts

1976 *Bicentennial Crafts*, San Diego State University, San Diego, California

1976 *National Invitational Crafts Exhibition*, Krannert Art Museum, University of Illinois, Urbana, Illinois

1976 *Textiles, Past & Prologue*, Greenville County Museum of Art, Greenville, South Carolina

1976 *Vannerie Traditionelle D'Afrique Et D'Asie Et Nouvelle Vannerie*, Lausanne, Switzerland

1976 *Stuctuur in Textiel*, Stedelijk Museum, Amsterdam, Netherlands

1977 *Wall Hangings: The New Classicism*, The Museum of Modern Art, New York, New York

1977 *The Dyer's Art: Ikat, Batik, Plangi*, Museum of Contemporary Crafts, New York, New York

1977 *The Object as Poet*, National Museum of American Art, Renwick Gallery, Smithsonian Institution, Washington, DC

1977 *Fiber Works: The Americans and Japan*, National Museum of Modern Art, Kyoto, Japan

1978 *Fiber: New Directions 1978*, Cheney Cowles Memorial Museum, Spokane, Washington

1978 *Martex; A Changing Exhibition of Contemporary Art* University Art Museum, Berkeley, California

1981 *The Art Fabric: Mainstream*, San Francisco Museum of Modern Art, San Francisco, California

1981 *Fiber '81: An Exhibition of Contemporary Textiles*, Desaisset Gallery, University of Santa Clara, Santa Clara, California

1981 *Old Traditions/ New Directions*, The Textile Museum, Washington, DC

1981 *Nouvelle Vannerie*, Musee des Arts Decoratifs, Lausanne Switzerland

1982 *The Jacquard Loom*, Museum of Art, Rhode Island School of Design, Providence, Rhode Island

1982 *Basketry Today*, Mather Gallery, Case Western Reserve, Cleveland, Ohio

1983 *USA Today*, USA Today Gallery, Arlington, Virginia

1983 *Art: The Textile Reference*, Artifacts Gallery, Indianapolis, Indiana

1984 *Re-opening Exhibit: Selections from the Permanent Collection, Architecture and Design*, The Museum of Modern Art, New York, New York

1984 *Design in America: The Cranbrook Vision*, Cranbrook Academy of Art Museum, Bloomfield Hills, Michigan

1984 *Damask Exhibition*, Cooper Hewitt Museum, Smithsonian Institution, New York, New York

1984 *The Modern Basket: At the Edge*, Visual Arts Center of Alaska, Anchorage, Alaska

1984 *The New Basket: A Vessel of the Future*, Brainard Art Gallery, State University College, Potsdam, New York

1985 *California Crafts XIV: Living Treasures of California*, Crocker Museum, Sacramento, California

1985 *Basketry Today*, University of Wisconsin, Green Bay, Wisconsin

1986 *Fiber R/Evolution*, Milwaukee Art Museum, University Art Museum, University of Wisconsin—Milwaukee, Milwaukee, Wisconsin

1986 *Legends in Fiber*, Octagon Center for the Arts, Ames, Iowa

1986 *Craft Today: Poetry of the Physical*, American Crafts Museum, New York, New York

1987 *Knots and Nets*, Herbert F. Johnson Museum of Art, Cornell University, Ithaca, New York

1987 *The Modern Basket*: A Redefinition, Pittsburg Center for the Arts, Pittsburg, Pennsylvania

1987 *Baskets as Sculpture*, Miller/Brown Gallery, San Francisco, California

1987 *Ideas and Images Through Paper*, David Fine Gallery, Portland State University, Portland, Oregon

1987 *Art in the Craft Media*, Bellas Artes Gallery, Santa Fe, New Mexico

1987 *Interlacing: the Elemental Fabric*, American Craft Museum, New York, New York

1987 *Baskets from Five Continents*, Wadsworth Atheneum, Hartford Connecticut

1988 *Frontiers in Fiber: The Americans*, North Dakota Museum of Art, Grand Forks, North Dakota

1988 *American Baskets: the Eighties*, Randolph Gallery, Chicago Public Library Cultural Center, Chicago, Illinois

1988 *Focus: American Basketry*, Katie Gingrass Gallery, Milwaukee, Wisconsin

1988 *Contemporary American Hand '88*, Katie Gingrass Gallery, Milwaukee, Wisconsin

1988 *Craft Today, USA*, American Craft Museum, New York, New York

1988 *The Tactile Vessel: New Basket Forms*, Erie Art Museum, Erie, Pennsylvania

1988 *Basketry '88 / Evolution into Sculpture*, WITA Gardiner Gallery, San Diego, California

1988 *Material Departures*, The Walter Gallery, Santa Monica, California

1989 *Artful Objects: Recent American Craft*, Fort Wayne Museum of Art, Fort Wayne, Indiana

1989 *Fiber Concepts*, Arizona State University, Tempe, Arizona

SELECTED COLLECTIONS

American Craft Museum, New York, New York

Arizona State University, Tempe, Arizona

Art Institute of Chicago, Chicago, Illinois

The Brooklyn Museum, Brooklyn, New York

California State Fair, Sacramento, California

The Council House, International Conference Center of S.C. Johnson & Son, Inc., Racine, Wisconsin

Cranbrook Academy of Art Museum, Bloomfield Hills, Michigan

The Detroit Institute of Arts, Detroit, Michigan

Erie Art Museum, Erie, Pennsylvania

Indiana University Art Museum, Bloomington, Indiana

The Oakland Museum, Oakland, California

Mansfield State College, Art Museum Collection, Mansfield, Massachusetts

The Metropolitan Museum of Art, New York, New York

Milwaukee Art Museum, Milwaukee, Wisconsin

Musee Des Arts Decoratifs de Montreal, Montreal, Canada

The Museum of Modern Art, New York, New York

National Museum of American Art, Renwick Gallery, Smithsonian Institution, Washington, DC

Stedelijk Museum, Amsterdam, Netherlands

Trondheim Museum, Trondheim, Norway

University of Illinois, Champaign-Urbana, Champaign, Illinois

University of Nebraska, Lincoln, Nebraska

Wadsworth Atheneum, Hartford, Connecticut

Women's College, University of North Carolina, Greensboro, North Carolina

ROSSBACH RETROSPECTIVE SUPPORT GROUP

Mr. and Mrs. Leonard I. Abel
Mr. and Mrs. Ronald D. Abramson
Ms. Karen Johnson Boyd
The Rau Foundation:
   Mr. and Mrs. John Alton Boyer
Mr. and Mrs. E. Patrick Coady
Ms. Jean Efron
Mr. and Mrs. Carl S. Gewirz
Mr. and Mrs. Jack Kay
Mr. and Mrs. Marvin L. Kay

WRITINGS BY ED ROSSBACH

1938   Making Marionettes. Harcourt, Brace, New York.

1948   Hand-Weaving as an Art Form. *Craft Horizons*, vol. 8, no. 23 (Nov.), pp. 20-21. American Craftsmen's Council, New York.

1950   Designing for Table and Floor Looms. *Craft Horizons*, vol. 10, no. 3 (Autumn), pp. 40-41. American Craftsmen's Council, New York.

1953   Contemporary Batiks. *Craft Horizons*, vol. 13, no. 6 (Nov./Dec.), pp. 19-21. American Craftsmen's Council, New York.

1954   Design in Handwoven Screens Part I. *Handweaver & Craftsman*, vol. 6, no. 1, (Winter), pp. 16-19, 53. New York.

1955   Weaving for Screens: a Tactile Approach. *Craft Horizons,* vol. 15, no. 1 (Jan./Feb.), pp. 26-29. American Craftsmen's Council, New York.

1955   Design in Handwoven Screens Part II. *Handweaver & Craftsman*, vol. 6, no. 3 (Summer), pp. 16-18. New York.

1966   with Bernard Kester, Trude Guermonprez and Katherine Westphal, Textiles. *Craft Horizons*, vol. 26, no. 3 (June), pp. 32-34. American Craftsmen's Council, New York.

1971   Thoughts on Jack Lenor Larsen and the Textile Horizon. *Craft Horizons*, vol. 31, no. 2 (April), p. 13. American Crafts Council, New York.

1971   The Mats of Nabeul. *Craft Horizons*, vol. 31, no. 2 (April), pp. 33-34, 57-61. American Crafts Council, New York.

1972   Objects: USA Revisited. *Craft Horizons*, vol. 23, no. 4 (Aug.), pp. 38-39. American Crafts Council, New York.

1973   Baskets as Textile Art. Van Nostrand Reinhold Company, New York.

1973   The Hand-Blocked Textiles of Persia. *Craft Horizons*, vol. 33, no. 1 (Feb.), pp. 54-55, 78-79. American Crafts Council, New York.

1973   Workshop: Plaiting Baskets with Plant Material. *Craft Horizons*, vol. 33, no. 6 (Dec.), pp. 28-30. American Crafts Council, New York.

1974   The Fiber Game. *Craft Horizons*, vol. 34, no. 6 (Dec.), p. 49. American Crafts Council, New York.

1976   The New Basketry. Van Nostrand Reinhold Company, New York.

1976   Ed Rossbach Says. *Craft Horizons*, vol. 36, no. 3 (June), pp. 23-25, 27, 80. American Crafts Council, New York.

1976   Trude Guermonprez 1910-1976. *Craft Horizons*, vol. 36, no. 4 (Aug.), p. 10. American Crafts Council, New York.

1978   One Man's Bias on Surface Design. *Craft Horizons*, vol. 38, no. 2 (April), pp. 28-35. American Crafts Council, New York.

1978   Thoughts Inspired by the Exhibition. *In* Point of Contact, Fiberworks, Berkeley.

1980   The Art of Paisley. Van Nostrand Reinhold Company, New York.

1981   The Art of Paisley. American Fabrics and Fashions, no. 121 (Winter), pp. 20-25. Doric Publishing Company, New York.

1981   with Katherine Westphal, Filaments of the Imagination. *American Craft*, vol. 41, no. 3 (June/July), pp. 10-15. American Craft Council, New York.

1981   Answers without Questions. *In* Matter, Memory, Meaning (Gyongy Laky, ed.), p. 6. Honolulu Academy of Arts.

1982   Fiber Artists and the Jacquard Loom. *American Craft*, vol. 42, no. 1 (Feb./Mar.), pp. 6-10. American Craft Council, New York.

1982   with Jan Janeiro, Excerpts from a Conversation with Ed Rossbach. Fiberworks, Center for the Textile Arts, Spring Session Schedule, p. 6. Berkeley.

1982   Fiber in the Forties. *American Craft*, vol. 42, no. 5 (Oct./Nov.), pp. 15-19. American Craft Council, New York.

1982   The Glitter and Glamour of Dorothy Liebes. *American Craft*, vol. 42, no. 6 (Dec./Jan.), pp. 8-12. American Craft Council, New York.

1983   Mary Atwater and the Revival of American Traditional Weaving. *American Craft*, vol. 43, no. 2 (April/May), pp. 22-26. American Craft Council, New York.

1983   In the Bauhaus Mode: Anni Albers. *American Craft*, vol. 43, no. 6 (Dec./Jan), pp. 7-11. American Craft Council, New York.

1983   Introduction. *In* Artists in Fiber: 1981-1983, National Endowment for the Arts Fellowship Winners, Fiberworks, Berkeley.

1984   Thinking about Historical Baskets. *Fiberarts*, vol. 11, no. 1 (Jan./Feb.), pp. 32-33, 70. Lark Communications, Asheville, N.C.

1984   Marianne Strengell. *American Craft*, vol. 44, no. 2 (April/May), pp. 8-11. American Craft Council, New York.

1984   The Creative Process: Ed Rossbach. *Fiberarts*, vol. 11, no. 6 (Nov./Dec.), pp. 60-61. Lark Communications, Asheville, N.C.

1986   The Nature of Basketry. Schiffer Publishing, Exton, Penn.

1986   Ed Rossbach. *In* The Basketmaker's Art: Contemporary Baskets and their Makers (Rob Pulleyn, ed.), pp. 14-19. Lark Books, Asheville, N.C.

REFERENCES CITED

Albers, Anni, et al.
1948   Fabrics. *Arts and Architecture* (March, pp. 32-38. Los Angeles.

Albright, Thomas
1985   Art in the San Francisco Bay Area 1945-1980. University of California Press, Berkeley.

Alloway, Lawrence
1975   Topics in American Art Since 1945. Norton, New York.

1976   Robert Rauschenberg's Development. *In* Robert Rauschenberg. Smithsonian Institution Press, Washington.

American Fabrics
1965   American Fabrics Knitting Chart. No. 70 (Winter), pp. 80-81. New York.

Anonymous
1966   Museum West. *Craft Horizons*, vol. 26, no. 4 (Jul./Aug.), p. 39. New York.

Atwater, Mary Meigs
1928   The Shuttle-Craft Book of American Handweaving. The Macmillan Company, New York. Revised edition 1951.

Bath, Virginia Churchill
1974   Lace. Henry Regnery Company, Chicago.

Blasdel, Gregg N.
1968   The Grass-Roots Artists. *Art in America*, vol. 56 (Sept./Oct.), pp. 24-41. Des Moines, Iowa.

Boyer, Ruth M.
1978   Anna Hadwick Gayton (1899-1977). *Journal of American Folklore*, vol. 91, no. 361 (July-Sept.), pp. 834-841. Washington.

Brandford, Charles T.
1952   Bauhaus Weimar 1919-25, Dessau 1925-28. Charles T. Brandford Company, Boston.

Brandford, Joanne Segal
1976   The North American Basket 1790-1976. Craft Center, Worcester, Mass.

Brite, Jane Fassett
1986   Fiber R/Evolution. Milwaukee Art Museum and University Art Museum, The University of Wisconsin-Milwaukee.

Brookfield Craft Center
1974   Fiber Forms: Past and Present. Brookfield, Conn.

Campbell, David R.
1960   Designer-Craftsmen USA 1960. *Craft Horizons*, vol. 20, no.4 (July/Aug.), pp. 12-27. New York.

Centre International de la Tapisserie
1967   3e Biennale Internationale de la Tapisserie. Musee Cantonal des Beaux-Arts, Lausanne.

Chamberlain, Marcia and Candace Crockett
1974   Beyond Weaving. Watson-Guptill Publications, New York.

Clark, Garth
1979   A Century of Ceramics in the United States 1878-1978. E.P. Dutton, New York.

Constantine, Mildred and Jack Lenor Larsen
1969   Wall Hangings. Museum of Modern Art, New York.

1973   Beyond Craft: The Art Fabric. Van Nostrand Reinhold Company, New York.

1981   The Art Fabric: Mainstream. Van Nostrand Reinhold Company, New York.

Crommelin, Liesbeth
1976   Structuur in Textiel. Stedelijk Museum, Amsterdam.

Curtis, Cathy
1982   Fiberworks: When Everything Was Possible. The Goodfellow Review of Crafts, vol. 10, issue 4 (July/Aug.), pp. 9-10. Berkeley.

Cyrus, Ulla
1956   Manual of Swedish Handweaving. Charles T. Brandford Company, Boston.

Elliott, Lillian
1986   Today's Baskets: The Development of a Contemporary Aesthetic. *In* The Basketmaker's Art: Contemporary Baskets and Their Makers (Rob Pulleyn, ed.), pp. 9-13. Lark Books, Asheville, N.C.

Emery, Irene
1966   The Primary Structures of Fabrics: an Illustrated Classification. The Textile Museum, Washington.

Glashausser, Suellen and Carol Westfall
1976   Plaiting Step-by-Step. Watson-Guptill Publications, New York.

Goodall, Donald
1966   Craftsmen USA '66, Southwest Region. *Craft Horizons*, vol. 26, no. 2 (March/April), pp. 32-34, 50-51. New York.

Guggenheim Museum
1966   Systemic Painting. New York.

Hagberg, Marilyn
1972   Ed Rossbach: Planar Weavings and Photographic Pieces, Anneberg Gallery, San Francisco, California; September 14-October 14. *Craft Horizons*, vol. 32, no. 6, p. 55. New York.

Hall, Julie
1977   Tradition and Change: The New American Craftsman. E.P. Dutton, New York.

Hammel, Lisa
1988   A Passel of Baskets. *Town and Country*, vol. 142, no. 5099, pp. 167-170. New York.

Harcourt, Raoul d'
1962   Textiles of Ancient Peru and Their Techniques. (Trans. by Sadie Brown; Grace G. Denny and Carolyn M. Osborne, eds.). University of Washington Press, Seattle.

Harrison, Margaret W.
1948   Lila Morris O'Neale: 1886-1948. *American Anthropologist*, n.s., vol. 50, pt. 1, pp. 657-665. Menasha, Wisc.

Harvey, Virginia I.
1972   Color and Design in Macrame. Van Nostrand Reinhold Company, New York.

1974   The Techniques of Basketry. Van Nostrand Reinhold Company, New York.

Held, Shirley E.
1973   Weaving: A Handbook for Fiber Craftsmen. Holt, Rinehart and Winston, New York.

1978   Weaving: A Handbook of the Fiber Arts. Holt, Rinehart and Winston, New York.

Hickman, Pat
n.d.   Telephone interview with author Lia Cook, June 1989.

Jacob, Mary Jane
1985   Anni Albers: A Modern Weaver as Artist. *In* The Woven and Graphic Art of Anni Albers (Lloyd E. Herman, ed.), pp. 65-105. Smithsonian Institution Press, Washington.

Janeiro, Jan
1988   Piece Work: The World of Katherine Westphal. *American Craft*, vol. 48, no. 4 (Aug./Sept.), pp. 32-39. New York.

Janson, H.W.
1962   History of Art. Prentice Hall, Englewood Cliffs, N.J. and Harry N. Abrams, N.Y.

Kaufman, Ruth
1968   The New American Tapestry. Reinhold Book Corp., New York.

Kaufmann, Edgar, Jr.
1950   What is Modern Design? The Museum of Modern Art, New York.

Kuspit, Donald
1989   The Will to Unintelligibility in Modern Art: Abstraction Reconsidered. *New Art Examiner* vol. 17 (May) pp. 26-29. Chicago.

Laky, Gyongy
n.d.   Telephone interview with author Lia Cook, April 1989.

Larsen, Jack Lenor
1978   Rossbachs. *Surface Design*, vol. 2, no. 2 (Spring), pp. 30-31. Greenville, N.C.

Larsen, Jack Lenor with Alice Adams and Robert Riley
1961   Fabrics International. *Craft Horizons*, vol. 21, no. 5 (Sept./Oct.), pp. 3-50. New York. Also published separately.

Larsen, Jack Lenor with Alfred Buhler, Bronwyn and Garrett Solyom
1977   The Dyer's Art: Ikat, Batik, Plangi. Van Nostrand Reinhold, New York.

Larsen, Jack Lenor, Edgar Kaufmann, Jr. and Charles Forberg
1964   Milan: The Triennale, United States. *Craft Horizons*, vol. 24, no. 5 (Sept./Oct.), pp. 26-31. New York.

Larsen, Jack Lenor with Betty Freudenheim
1987   Interlacing: The Elemental Fabric. Kodansha International, Tokyo, New York and San Francisco.

Life
1972   A New Form Fit to be Tied: Rope Art. Vol. 73, no. 22 (Dec. 1), pp. 86-89. New York.

Loir, Helene
1935   Le tissage du raphia au Congo Belge. *Annales du Musee du Congo Belge*, Ethnographie, serie 3, vol. 3, fasc. 1 (Oct.). Tervueren, Belgium.

Malarcher, Patricia
1984   What Makes a Basket a Basket? *Fiberarts*, vol. 11, no. 1 (Jan./Feb.), pp. 34-41. Asheville, N.C.

Marcoux, Alice
1982   Jacquard Textiles. Museum of Art, Rhode Island School of Design, Providence.

Mare, Dominic di
n.d.   Interview with author Nancy Corwin, Tiburon, Calif., 5 July 1989.

Marein, Shirley
1977   New York/Fiber. *Craft Horizons*, vol. 37, no. 5 (Oct.), pp. 52-53. New York.

Mayer, Barbara
1988   Contemporary American Craft Art: A Collector's Guide. Peregrine Smith Books, Salt Lake City.

McQueen, John
n.d.   Telephone interview with author Lia Cook, 16 July 1989.

Miller, Lea Van Puymbroeck
1948   The Judges Award. *Craft Horizons*, vol. 8, no. 19 (Feb.), pp. 22-23. New York.

Moore, Eudorah M.
1968   California Design X. Pasadena Art Museum, Pasadena. The Ward Ritchie Press.

Moseley, Spencer
1966   Ed Rossbach: Textiles. Museum West of the American Craftsmen's Council, San Francisco.

Nagle, Virginia (ed.)
1960   American Weaving. *Design Quarterly*, no. 48-49, Walker Art Center, Minneapolis.

Naylor, Gillian
1968   The Bauhaus. Studio Vista, London.

Nordness, Lee

1970   Objects: U.S.A. The Viking Press, New York.

1980   The Council House, The International Conference Center of the S.C. Johnson & Son, Inc., Racine, Wisconsin. Perimeter Press.

Oka, Hideyuki

1967   How to Wrap Five Eggs. Weatherhill, Tokyo and Harper and Row, New York.

O'Neale, Lila

1932   Yurok-Karok Basket Weavers. *University of California Publications in American Archaeology and Ethnology*, vol. 32, no. 1. Berkeley.

1945   Textiles of Highland Guatemala. Carnegie Institution of Washington.

1946   Mochica (Early Chimu) and Other Peruvian Twill Fabrics. *Southwestern Journal of Anthropology*, vol. 2, no. 3 (Autumn), pp. 269-294. Albuquerque.

O'Neale, Lila and Bonnie Jean Clark

1948   Textile Periods in Ancient Peru III: The Gauze Weaves. *University of California Publications in American Archaeology and Ethnology*, vol. 40, no. 4. Berkeley.

O'Neale, Lila M. and Alfred L. Kroeber

1930   Textile Periods in Ancient Peru. *University of California Publications in American Archaeology and Ethnology*, vol. 28, no. 2. Berkeley.

Park, Betty

1979   An Interview with John McQueen. *Fiberarts*, vol. 6, no. 1 (Jan./Feb.), pp. 21-25. Asheville, N.C.

Parks, Dennis

1971   Katherine Westphal—Ed Rossbach—Marvin Lipofsky, Jewish Community Center Gallery, San Diego, California; December 2-January 3. *Craft Horizons*, vol. 31, no. 3 (June), p. 68. New York.

Peterson, Lisa Lee

n.d.   Telephone interview with author Lia Cook, 16 July 1989.

Press, Nancy Neumann

1988   Knots and Nets. Herbert F. Johnson Museum of Art, Cornell University, Ithaca, N.Y.

Pulleyn, Rob (ed.)

1986   The Basketmaker's Art: Contemporary Baskets and Their Makers. Lark Books, Asheville, N.C.

Rose, Barbara

1975   American Art Since 1900. Holt, Rinehart and Winston, New York.

Rossbach, Ed

1948   Hand-Weaving as an Art Form. *Craft Horizons*, vol. 8, no. 23 (Nov.), pp. 20-21. New York.

1950   Designing for Table and Floor Looms. *Craft Horizons*, vol. 10, no. 3 (Autumn), pp. 40-41. New York.

1954   Design in Handwoven Screens Part I. *Handweaver & Craftsman*, vol. 6, no. 1, (Winter), pp. 16-19, 53. New York.

1955a   Weaving for Screens: a Tactile Approach. *Craft Horizons*, vol. 15, no. 1 (Jan./Feb.), pp. 26-29. New York.

1955b   Design in Handwoven Screens Part II. *Handweaver & Craftsman*, vol. 6, no. 3 (Summer), pp. 16-18. New York.

1971   Thoughts on Jack Lenor Larsen and the Textile Horizon. *Craft Horizons*, vol. 31, no. 2 (April), p. 13. New York.

1973a   Baskets as Textile Art. Van Nostrand Reinhold Company, New York.

1973b   Workshop: Plaiting Baskets with Plant Material. *Craft Horizons*, vol. 33, no. 6 (Dec.), pp. 28-30. New York.

1976a   The New Basketry. Van Nostrand Reinhold Company, New York.

1976b   Ed Rossbach Says. *Craft Horizons*, vol. 36, no. 3 (June), pp. 23-25, 27, 80. New York.

1978   One Man's Bias on Surface Design. *Craft Horizons*, vol. 38, no. 2 (April), pp. 28-35. New York.

1980   The Art of Paisley. Van Nostrand Reinhold Company, New York.

1981   Answers without Questions. *In* Matter, Memory,

Meaning (Gyongy Laky, ed.), p. 6. Honolulu Academy of Arts.

1982a Fiber Artists and the Jacquard Loom. *American Craft*, vol. 42, no. 1 (Feb./Mar.), pp. 6-10. New York.

1982b Fiber in the Forties. *American Craft*, vol. 42, no. 5 (Oct./Nov.), pp. 15-19. New York.

1982c The Glitter and Glamour of Dorothy Liebes. *American Craft*, vol. 42, no. 6 (Dec./Jan.), pp. 8-12. New York.

1983 Mary Atwater and the Revival of American Traditional Weaving. *American Craft*, vol. 43, no. 2 (April/May), pp. 22-26. New York.

1984a Thinking about Historical Baskets. *Fiberarts*, vol. 11, no. 1 (Jan./Feb.), pp. 32-33, 70. Asheville, N.C.

1984b Marianne Strengell. *American Craft*, vol. 44, no. 2 (April/May), pp. 8-11. New York.

1984c The Creative Process: Ed Rossbach. *Fiberarts*, vol. 11, no. 6 (Nov./Dec.), pp. 60-61. Asheville, N.C.

1986 The Nature of Basketry. Schiffer Publishing, Exton, Penn.

n.d.a The Weaver's Secret Book. Unpublished artist's book, 1977.

n.d.b Interview with Jim Carlson and unidentified woman. Tape recording, Oral History Collection, American River College, Sacramento, Calif., Feb. 1981.

n.d.c Interview with author Nancy Corwin, Berkeley, 18 June 1986.

n.d.d Interview with Jane Brite, 1986. Tape transcription.

n.d.e Charles Edmund Rossbach: Artist, Mentor, Professor, Writer. Interview with Harriet Nathan conducted in 1983, Copy 14, Fiber Arts Oral History Series, Regional Oral History Office, The Bancroft Library, University of California, Berkeley, 1987.

n.d.f Interviews with author Ann Rowe, Berkeley, 10-12 January 1989.

n.d.g Letter to author Ann Rowe, 19 January 1989.

n.d.h Interview with authors Rebecca Stevens, Jane Brite, and Ann Rowe, Washington, 16 May 1989.

n.d.i Written answers to questions from Jane Brite, 5 June 1989. Copy on file at The Textile Museum, Washington.

n.d.j Letter to author Ann Rowe, 28 August 1989.

n.d.k Telephone conversation with author Rebecca Caldwell, 31 August 1989.

Rossbach, Katherine
1970 Ed Rossbach: A Tribe of Baskets. *Craft Horizons*, vol. 30, no. 5 (Oct.), pp. 16-17. New York.

Roth, Henry Ling
1918 Studies in Primitive Looms. Bankfield Museum, Halifax.

Rowe, Ann Pollard
1985 After Emery: Further Considerations of Fabric Classification and Terminology. *The Textile Museum Journal*, vol. 23 (1984), pp. 53-71. Washington.

Rowley, Kathleen
1984 Words in Fiber. *Fiberarts*, vol. 11, no. 2 (March/April), pp. 66-69. Asheville, N.C.

Selz, Peter
1985 Art in a Turbulent Era. UMI Press, Ann Arbor.

Shorr, Mimi
1972 Fiber Sculpture. *Saturday Review*, vol. 55 (20 May), pp. 57-61. New York.

Smith, Dido
1970 Ed Rossbach, Lee Nordness Galleries, New York; May 12-June 2. *Craft Horizons*, vol. 30, no. 4 (Aug.), p. 55. New York.

Smith, Paul J.
1972 Sculpture in Fiber. Museum of Contemporary Crafts, New York.

Smith, Paul J. and Edward Lucie-Smith
1986 Craft Today: Poetry of the Physical. American Craft Museum, New York.

Slivka, Rose (ed.)
1968 The Crafts of the Modern World. Horizon Press

Publishers, World Crafts Council, New York.

1976   The Object as Poet. Smithsonian Institution Press, Washington.

Steinberg, Leo
1972   Other Criteria. Oxford University Press, New York.

Stevens, Rebecca A.T.
1981   Old Traditions, New Directions. The Textile Museum, Washington.

Story, William E.
1972   Fiber Art by American Artists. Art Gallery, Ball State University, Muncie, Indiana.

Thurman, Christa C. Mayer
1983   Textiles. *In* Design in America: The Cranbrook Vision 1925-1950, pp. 172-211. Harry N. Abrams, Publishers, New York, in association with The Detroit Institute of Arts and The Metropolitan Museum of Art.

Tomkins, Calvin
1978   The Bride and the Bachelors. Penguin, New York.

Waller, Irene
1977   Textile Sculptures. Taplinger Publishing Company, New York.

Webb, Katy
n.d.   Telephone interview with author Lia Cook, May 1989.

West, Virginia
1982   Ed Rossbach: Embracing the Fabric of Art. *Fiberarts*, vol. 9, no. 1 (Jan.-Feb.), pp. 31-33. Asheville, N.C.

Westphal, Katherine
1976   Katherine Westphal Says. Craft Horizons, vol. 36, no. 3 (June), pp. 22, 26. New York.

White, Patrick
1986   The Painting as Artifact. Sioux City Art Center, Sioux City, Iowa.

Zeisler, Claire
n.d.   Interview with authors Rebecca Stevens and Jane Brite, Chicago, 21 September 1988.

Znamierowski, Nell
1970   Dorothy Liebes. Museum of Contemporary Crafts, New York.

THE AUTHORS

Jane Fassett Brite, Director/Curator of Walker's Point Center for the Arts in Milwaukee, Wisconsin, was the curator of Fiber R/Evolution in which she included Rossbach's work. She is Curator of the 1990 Rossbach Exhibition at The Textile Museum, Washington, D.C.

Lia Cook, fiber artist, is Professor of Art, Textile Department, California College of Arts and Crafts, Oakland, California.

Rebecca A. T. Stevens, Consulting Curator, Contemporary Textiles, at The Textile Museum, first worked with Rossbach in 1981 while curating an exhibition which included his work.

Nancy A. Corwin, Ph.D. in art history, writer and professor was awarded one of the first of two James Renwick Fellowships in American Crafts. She is writing a book on the history of fiber art in America since 1945.

Ann Pollard Rowe, Curator of Western Hemisphere Textiles at The Textile Museum since 1972, studied with Rossbach as a graduate student in the Design Department at the University of California at Berkeley in 1969-70, where she received her M.A.

Rebecca Caldwell is a writer, editor, and a former teacher of English, living in Washington, D.C. She has a Master of Arts in English and Drama from the University of Tennessee, Knoxville.

Due to technical problems at Lark Books the diacritical marks are not reproduced in this text. We regret any inconveniences or confusion this may cause the reader.